30-SECOND
PSYCHOLOGY

30-SECOND
PSYCHOLOGY

**The 50 most thought-provoking
psychology theories, each
explained in half a minute**

Editor
Christian Jarrett

Contributors
**Vaughan Bell
Moheb Costandi
Christian Jarrett
Dave Munger
Tom Stafford**

ICON

First published in the UK in 2011 by
Icon Books Ltd
Omnibus Business Centre
39–41 North Road, London N7 9DP
email: info@iconbooks.com
www.iconbooks.com

This book was conceived,
designed and produced by
Ivy Press
210 High Street, Lewes
East Sussex, BN7 2NS, UK
www.ivypress.co.uk

Creative Director **Peter Bridgewater**
Publisher **Jason Hook**
Editorial Director **Caroline Earle**
Art Director **Michael Whitehead**
Designer **Ginny Zeal**
Concept Design **Linda Becker**
Illustrator **Ivan Hissey**
Profiles & Glossaries Text **Nic Compton**
Assistant Editor **Jamie Pumfrey**

ISBN: 978-1-84831-261-6

Printed and bound in China

Colour origination by
Ivy Press Reprographics

10 9 8

CONTENTS

INTRODUCTION
Christian Jarrett

The familiarity of psychology's subject matter sets it apart from the other sciences. After school, few of us will set foot in a chemistry laboratory, we're unlikely to peer down a microscope and the closest that we'll get to a black hole is watching *Star Trek*. By contrast, we all have a mind of our own, and we spend every day interacting with others. So the focus of psychology – on minds and behaviour – is familiar to everyone. In a sense, we're all amateur psychologists.

However, we should be careful not to confuse familiarity with mastery. Just because we have our pet theories for other people's motives and actions, doesn't mean they are accurate. Psychology is about setting aside our intuitions and using the objective tools of science to discover how the mind really works, why people really behave the way they do.

Such an endeavour met resistance from the outset. Questions of the mind used to be the preserve of philosophy. And even after the first laboratories demonstrated the feasibility of a psychological science, a movement within the discipline argued that only observable behaviour, not inner thoughts, should be studied. The first section of this book, **Old School, New School**, charts how these arguments were resolved and how psychology became the thriving and respected science that it is today.

A topic that provokes particularly strident lay beliefs is that of child development. Just how does a screaming, helpless, newborn child mature into a fully formed, self-conscious adult? The section on **Growth & Change** introduces you to the pioneers

The mind turned inward
Psychology is the scientific study of ourselves and why we behave the way we do. Intuition is put on hold and cool-headed experimentation is the order of the day.

in this field and concludes with the theory of neuroplasticity – recognition that our brains are flexible and never stop changing and adapting until the day that we die.

A focus of psychology that is of extreme practical relevance is how to optimize the decisions people make for the good of themselves and society at large. **Decision Making & Emotions** provides an overview of some of the biases that affect our thinking. As you will see, emotions, as well as providing the foundation of our humanity, also influence our decisions and so the two topics are dealt with together.

Whether in gangs or companies, sports teams or political parties, we humans are intrinsically social, forever forming groups to serve our needs and interests. **Social Psychology** deals with the issues that naturally arise when we mix and merge, including leadership and prejudice. The chapter also features some of the most famous experiments in psychology including Zimbardo's insights into tyranny and Milgram's 'shocking' research on obedience.

The next two sections, **Ways We Differ** and **Disordered Minds,** feature theories that perhaps most closely resemble popular beliefs about psychology: from personality and intelligence to insanity and psychotherapy. The last section, **Thoughts & Language,** deals with those theories that delve inside our heads, beginning with the placebo effect—the power of the mind to affect the body – and ending with consciousness, the miracle and mystery of how flesh gives rise to mental life.

Each of the book's 50 entries provides a plain English 30-second introduction, a 3-second 'psyche' for when you're really in a rush, and a 3-minute analysis, which probes a little deeper. The chapters also include biographical profiles of some of the luminaries in this field, including Sigmund Freud and William James. Whether you choose to dip in or to study the book from cover to cover, you are about to learn about the most complex entity in the universe – the human mind. Have fun!

A new science

Psychology is relatively young – its first laboratories weren't established until the late nineteenth century. Yet there are already many important and controversial psychological theories. Allow our team of talented writers to introduce you to them.

OLD SCHOOL, NEW SCHOOL

OLD SCHOOL, NEW SCHOOL
GLOSSARY

anthropology The study of humankind. Areas covered include the origins and development of the human species, its biological characteristics, belief structures and social customs. Although the subject was discussed by Herodotus as long ago as 500 BC, it only became a discipline in its own right during the Renaissance, with the writings of Michel de Montaigne, René Descartes and Immanuel Kant. The term comes from the Greek *anthropos* (human) and *logos* (science) and was coined in Germany in the sixteenth century.

consciousness The totality of experience of which a person is aware at any one moment. This is a constantly shifting state, moving between current thought processes, memory, visual and aural stimuli and physical experiences. The US psychologist William James said consciousness was like a stream, constantly chopping and changing direction, but essentially continuous.

Ego According to Freud, this is the conscious, rational part of personality. He saw the human psyche as being made up of three parts: the Id, which seeks instant gratification, the Superego, which makes moral judgments, and the Ego, which mediates between the first two. It does so using the 'reality principle', which compels us to abide by current social norms. Freud said the Id was like a horse and the Ego like a man riding the horse and controlling its wilder instincts.

Id According to Freud, this is the instinctive, unconscious aspect of human personality that seeks immediate gratification. Its primitive impulses are restrained and controlled by the Ego. Although the Id is often associated with negative and antisocial behaviour, it is also responsible for instincts that are essential for our survival, such as hunger and thirst, as well as the reproductive urge.

neuroscience The study of the nervous system, including the brain functions and how they relate to human behaviour. Ultimately the task of neuroscientists is to discover the functions of all parts of the brain, what mental processes they perform and how they are affected by external stimuli. Once a branch of biology, it is now regarded as an interdisciplinary science which covers several other disciplines, such as psychology, medicine and computer science.

neurosis A mild mental disorder characterized by anxiety and phobias, but not so extreme that the patient suffers from delusions or hallucinations. According to Freud, the condition is part of the Ego's self-defence mechanism and is triggered by unresolved inner conflicts. Although once a common diagnosis, the term is no longer used in mainstream psychiatry, apart from specific use in psychoanalytic practice and theory.

neurotic A person who suffers from neurosis, or having the symptoms of neurosis. Symptoms include hysteria, obsessive-compulsiveness and a long list of phobias, such as agoraphobia (fear of having a panic attack in a public space) and arachnophobia (fear of spiders).

pathogenic Causing disease, or being capable of causing disease. From the Greek *pathos* (disease) and *genesis* (creation).

personality conflict A clash between different aspects of someone's personality. According to Freud, the primitive instincts of the Id are in constant conflict with the self-conscious moralizing of the Superego and have to be mediated by the rationalism of the Ego. If this conflict is unresolved, it can lead to neurosis.

primatology The study of primates. Although primatology is a separate discipline from psychology, there is some overlap in the study of social groups and aspects of personality.

stimulus error The tendency for patients, during 'introspection', to name the objects they were visualizing rather than describing what those objects meant to them. Thus, just stating the presence of an apple is less informative than describing the shape and colour of the apple and what feelings they evoke. Introspection was used in the early days of psychiatry to describe a patient's conscious mind.

Superego According to Freud, that part of the personality that makes moral judgments and acts as our conscience. The Superego is mainly unconscious and formed through the internalization of one's parents' and society's moral codes. An over-strong Superego can lead a person to be moralistic and uncompromising towards other people.

WUNDT'S INTROSPECTION

the 30-second theory

RELATED THEORIES
See also
WATSON'S BEHAVIOURISM
Page 16
PSYCHOANALYSIS
Page 18

Are you sitting comfortably?

Now tell me, what are the contents of your conscious mind right now? This is a version of introspection – the research tool favoured by psychology's founding fathers in the late nineteenth century. As William James noted in his 1890 book *The Principles of Psychology*, 'The word introspection needs hardly to be defined – it means, of course, looking into our own minds and reporting what we there discover.' Practitioners in Wilhelm Wundt's laboratory at the University of Leipzig – widely accepted as the world's first experimental psychology lab – were expected to undergo lengthy training in the method. One aim was to break conscious experience down into its constituent parts. Although the technique sounds straightforward enough, methodological arguments broke out among its early pioneers. Edward Titchener, a British psychologist and former student of Wundt's, proposed a particularly strict system designed to avoid what he called 'stimulus error', in which, faced with a stimulus such as a table, the 'introspectionist' reports the mere presence of the table, rather than the raw sensory experiences provoked by its colour, size, position and constitution.

3-SECOND PSYCHE
The favoured research method of psychology's founding fathers was introspection – reporting the contents of one's own consciousness.

3-MINUTE ANALYSIS
Introspection as a formal technique fell out of favour with the rise of behaviourism, and with the growing recognition that many of our mental processes are beyond conscious access. However, any time a research participant reports how they are feeling or describes their sensory perceptions – as often happens as part of many modern psychology experiments – they are in effect introspecting.

3-SECOND BIOGRAPHIES
WILLIAM JAMES
1842–1910

EDWARD TITCHENER
1867–1927

WILHELM WUNDT
1832–1920

30-SECOND TEXT
Christian Jarrett

No one has direct access to your mind like you do. That's why introspection remains a valid technique even after the invention of brain scanners.

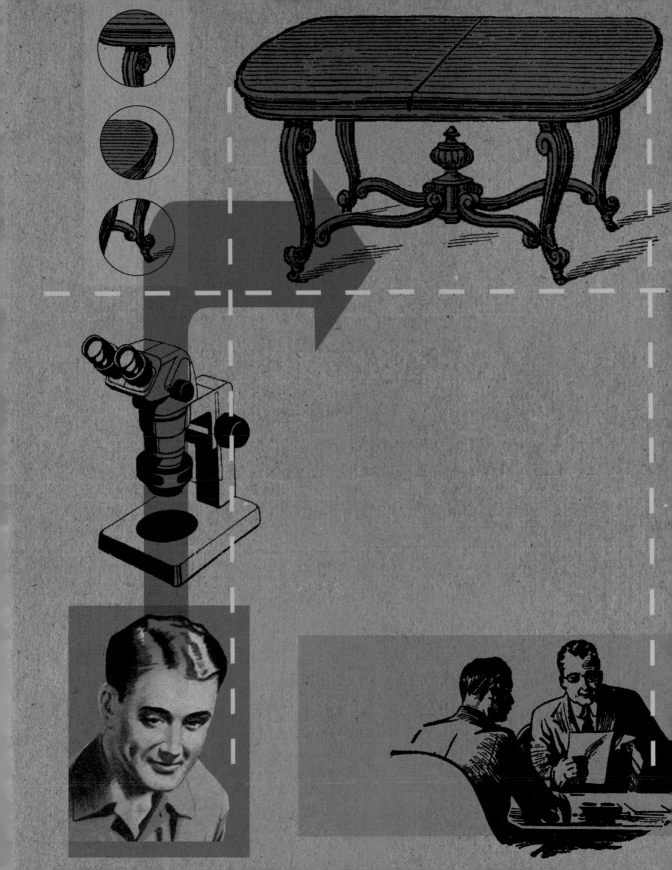

WATSON'S BEHAVIOURISM

the 30-second theory

3-SECOND PSYCHE
The only reliable evidence is something you can measure directly. For psychology this means we should only talk about behaviour, not about mental states.

3-MINUTE ANALYSIS
Modern psychology rejects the core idea of behaviourism (that it is impossible to scientifically discuss the structure of the mind). Despite this, many aspects of behaviourism remain central to modern psychology. These include the emphasis on recording objective measures in controlled experiments, the common study of psychological phenomena in non-human animals as well as in humans and psychologists' keen interest in learning.

Early psychologists investigated thinking by inspecting their own thoughts and the reports of the thoughts of others. The behaviourists rejected this method. Science, they argued, must be based on data that everyone can agree on, something reliable and objectively measurable. This means abandoning talk and reports of thoughts, and concentrating on simple behaviours. Rather than rely on subjective impressions, behaviourists conducted experiments in which the inputs ('stimuli') were controlled and the outputs ('responses') were measured. They hoped that from these experiments the relationship between the two could be inferred, with no need to worry about the intervening black box of the mind. For example, a rat in a cage would get a food reward every third time it pressed a lever. By recording the number of times that the rat pressed the lever, over time you could get an objective record of its rate of learning. Like this example, the most famous findings of behaviourism are about fundamental learning mechanisms that describe how associations with stimuli and responses are learned due to repetition or reward. The emphasis on simple behaviours allowed the behaviourists to develop theories that applied to non-human animals as well as humans.

RELATED THEORIES
See also
WUNDT'S INTROSPECTION
Page 14

THE COGNITIVE REVOLUTION
Page 22

PAVLOV'S DOGS
Page 134

3-SECOND BIOGRAPHIES
CLARK L. HULL
1884–1952

B.F. SKINNER
1904–1990

EDWARD THORNDIKE
1874–1949

EDWARD C. TOLMAN
1886–1959

JOHN B. WATSON
1878–1958

30-SECOND TEXT
Tom Stafford

The behaviourists were uninterested in the 'black box' of the mind, choosing to focus instead only on what is outwardly observable.

PSYCHOANALYSIS

the 30-second theory

Sigmund Freud conceived of and developed the concept of psychoanalysis during the late nineteenth and early twentieth centuries as a means of understanding behaviour. Freud believed that personality consists of three components: the Id, which is governed by pleasure and seeks immediate gratification; the Ego, which is concerned with making rational decisions; and the Superego, which makes moral judgments. The Ego is pulled to and fro by the Id and Superego, giving rise to personality conflicts. When the Ego is overwhelmed by the Id's demands, we become neurotic, and when it gives in to them, the Superego punishes the Ego with guilt. The Ego copes with these conflicting demands by means of neuroses and dreams, which fulfil the Id's suppressed desires, and with defence mechanisms such as repression and denial, which reduce anxiety. These mechanisms can be pathogenic, however, and are a major cause of mental illness. Alfred Adler and Carl Jung also contributed to psychoanalysis, but parted ways with Freud in the 1910s. Jung disagreed with him about the structure of personality, while Adler emphasized the importance of social factors in development, and believed that people are motivated by self-preservation, the will to power and a drive to affirm their personalities. Both also rejected Freud's emphasis on sexuality.

3-SECOND PSYCHE
Unconscious motivating forces play a central role in shaping our behaviour, but are also the primary cause of mental illness.

3-MINUTE ANALYSIS
The main criticisms of Freud's theories are that they are unfalsifiable and cannot be used to make predictions about outcomes of treatment. His patients were unrepresentative of the general population, and the fact that he treated very few children invalidates to a degree his theory of personality development. Freud has also been accused of distorting evidence to make it fit his theories. Nevertheless, his work remains highly influential, in both psychiatry and popular culture.

RELATED THEORY
See also
BIRTH ORDER
Page 36

3-SECOND BIOGRAPHIES
ALFRED ADLER
1870–1937

SIGMUND FREUD
1856–1939

CARL JUNG
1875–1961

30-SECOND TEXT
Moheb Costandi

It's all in the unconscious mind. Could your recurring dreams of a bed be a Freudian sign of sexual frustration?

1856
Born Sigismund Freud,
Freiberg, Moravia

1859
Family moves to Vienna

1881
M.D. from University of
Vienna

1886
Marries Martha Bernays

1900
Publishes *The
Interpretation of Dreams*

1902
Professor of
Neuropathology at
University of Vienna

1905
Publishes *Three Essays
on the Theory of
Sexuality*

1910
International
Psychoanalytic
Association founded

1923
Cancer diagnosed

1932
Receives Goethe Prize

1933
Books burned by the
Nazis

1938
Escapes to London

1939
Dies of cancer, London

SIGMUND FREUD

Anyone who says that sex didn't exist before the 1960s clearly hasn't read Sigmund Freud. Arguably the most influential psychologist that ever lived, Freud achieved global fame, if not notoriety, for his theories based on the idea that sex is the main driver of human behaviour. Not food. Not money. Not love. But primarily sex.

According to Freud, children go through three distinct phases of sexual development, defined by the body's erogenous zones: oral, anal and genital. A child as young as three years old, he suggested, has sexual feelings towards the parent of the opposite sex, which translates into jealousy of the parent of the same sex, either as an Oedipus or Electra complex. This is repressed, in the case of boys, by a fear of castration, which leads to him identifying with the father. Any problems along this journey will lead to fixations that will affect the person into adult life. When Freud published his theories of sexuality in 1905, it caused a furore and led to predictable accusations of sexual obsession.

But Freud, of course, wrote about a great deal more than sex. Perhaps his greatest legacy to the field of psychology was his exploration of the unconscious. Although other philosophers and psychologists, including Freud's mentors Josef Breuer and Jean-Martin Charcot, were investigating the unconscious through hypnosis, it was Freud's development of his concept of psychoanalysis (the 'talking cure') that really unlocked the secrets of the unconscious mind. And Freud's use of dreams to explore these unconscious desires has given rise to a whole genre of dream interpretation. Yet the image of the 'dirty old man of psychology' lingers on in the public imagination. It's no coincidence that while Pavlov is remembered for his dogs and Milgram is remembered for his obedience experiments, the inventor of psychoanalysis is remembered for his 'Freudian slip'.

THE COGNITIVE REVOLUTION

the 30-second theory

3-SECOND PSYCHE
Your mind is a machine for storing and processing information.

3-MINUTE ANALYSIS
Cognitivism remains at the heart of modern psychology. Although many psychologists still think of the mind in terms of information processing, advances in neuroscience have resulted in the investigation of the mind (the 'software') being combined with the investigation of the brain (the 'hardware') – a branch of psychology known as cognitive neuroscience. Moreover, evidence of neuroplasticity (how the brain alters over time) suggests that the computer metaphor has its limits. If the brain is a machine, it is a machine that changes itself.

Cognitivism is the attempt to understand the mind in terms of the information it processes and the forms in which it stores this information. Cognitivism is a rejection of psychoanalytic approaches, which try to understand the mind in terms of myth, and of behaviourist approaches, which try to understand the mind in terms of behaviour only. The start of the cognitive revolution is often dated to the appearance of an incendiary book review by linguist Noam Chomsky. Chomsky's review criticized the behaviourist psychologist B.F. Skinner's book *Verbal Behaviour*, in which he attempted to explain language learning using behaviourist principles. Cognitivism marked an evolution of behaviourism and is inspired by a computer metaphor of the mind. Computers have hardware and run software, which controls the flow of information between inputs and outputs and the reading and writing of information to the computer's memory. Cognitivists aim to investigate psychological 'software' – the mind – independently of the 'hardware' – the brain. Like the behaviourists, cognitivists are committed to the experimental method, but believe that they can prove something about what happens in between stimulus and response.

RELATED THEORIES
See also
WATSON'S BEHAVIOURISM
Page 16
NEUROPLASTICITY
Page 44
BROADBENT'S BOTTLENECK
Page 146

3-SECOND BIOGRAPHIES
DONALD BROADBENT
1926–1993
NOAM CHOMSKY
1928–

30-SECOND TEXT
Tom Stafford

The metaphor of the brain as a computer for processing and storing information has proved popular. However, it's best not to try to repair it with a wrench.

EVOLUTIONARY PSYCHOLOGY

the 30-second theory

3-SECOND PSYCHE
Evolution shaped your
mind to pass on your
genes to your offspring.

3-MINUTE ANALYSIS
Critics accuse evolutionary
psychologists of telling
'just-so stories' about
behaviour – plausible
tales that capture the
imagination but which
cannot be proved true
or false. Worse, critics
claim some people use
evolutionary arguments
to justify unfair or
implausible theories
about how society should
be organized. Despite
this, most psychologists
would agree that
psychology is part of
biology, and so must be
understood within the
framework of evolution
– they just disagree
about the extent to
which evolution is
directly relevant to
human behaviour.

The human body evolved

according to natural selection, and has many
things in common with the bodies of other
animals. Evolutionary psychology extends this
logic to the human mind. Like behaviourism,
the focus of evolutionary psychology is to find
common principles in the behaviour of humans
and animals. Evolutionary biologists have shown
how animals have evolved strategies to deal
with core activities such as food finding,
parenting, conflict resolution and mate
selection. Interesting work in evolutionary
psychology shows how these activities are
influenced by evolutionary necessity even
when carried out by supposedly rational
humans. There are two versions of evolutionary
psychology. A broad version of the theory
includes everybody who thinks about psychology
from an evolutionary perspective, including
anthropologists, biologists interested in
behaviour, primatologists and psychologists in
many areas. The second, more narrow, version
– sometimes distinguished by capital letters
('Evolutionary Psychology' or 'EP') – focuses
on applying ideas from evolutionary theory
to human reasoning and social behaviour,
and particularly to human sexual behaviour.

RELATED THEORIES
See also
EKMAN'S UNIVERSAL
EMOTIONS
Page 50
CHOMKSY'S UNIVERSAL
GRAMMAR
Page 138

3-SECOND BIOGRAPHIES
DAVID BUSS
1953–

LEDA COSMIDES
1957–

CHARLES DARWIN
1809–1882

STEVEN PINKER
1954–

JOHN TOOBY
1954–

30-SECOND TEXT
Tom Stafford

*Chimps, like humans,
form groups, laugh,
recognize themselves
in the mirror, and
use tools, suggesting
that we have a shared
evolutionary heritage.*

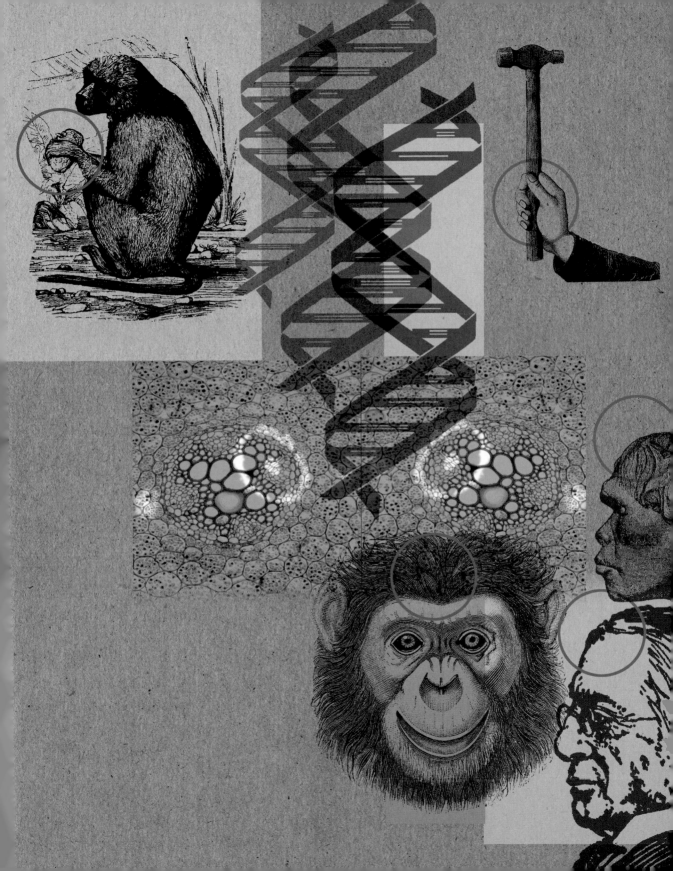

POSITIVE PSYCHOLOGY

the 30-second theory

3-SECOND PSYCHE
Psychology should spend less time focusing on people's mental distress and more time understanding and nurturing their strengths and virtues.

3-MINUTE ANALYSIS
Not everyone is enamoured of the positivity message. In 2009, the writer and activist Barbara Ehrenreich published a book entitled: *Bright-sided: How the Relentless Promotion of Positive Thinking Has Undermined America.* Among her targets for criticism, Ehrenreich cited research showing that a positive mental attitude has no bearing on survival rates for breast cancer. Writing from first-hand experience, Ehrenreich said that the pressure to be positive is an extra burden for cancer sufferers.

'That that don't kill me can only make me stronger.' So sang rapper Kanye West in his 2007 track 'Stronger'. Friedrich Nietzsche, the German philosopher, put it similarly in the nineteenth century when he wrote, 'What doesn't kill us makes us stronger.' Their words would make an ideal motto for positive psychology – a movement that was launched by University of Pennsylvania psychologist Martin Seligman in his presidential address to the American Psychological Association's annual convention in 1998. Seligman lamented the fact that psychology had for so long focused on mental ailments and distress. He called on the discipline to focus more on the positive – on people's strengths and virtues. Today the sub-discipline of positive psychology has its own journal, international organization and regular conferences. Research in positive psychology has uncovered tentative evidence that people's characters can be strengthened by adverse experiences, such as surviving a disaster or living with an illness. In the realm of work, productivity has been shown to rise when managers focus on their employees' strengths; in the context of therapy, researchers have found that it helps if therapists spend time considering their clients' strengths, not just their problems.

RELATED THEORIES
See also
SELIGMAN'S PREPARED LEARNING
Page 112

MASLOW'S HUMANISTIC PSYCHOLOGY
Page 122

3-SECOND BIOGRAPHY
MARTIN SELIGMAN
1942–

30-SECOND TEXT
Christian Jarrett

Look on the bright side – what doesn't kill you will only make you stronger. Positive psychology can be the key to deflecting life's little bullets.

GROWTH & CHANGE

behaviourist Someone who subscribes to behaviourism, a school of thought that believes psychology should concern itself only with visible, and therefore verifiable, behaviour, rather than invisible, and therefore unverifiable, thought processes. This approach contends that behaviour is mainly influenced by environmental stimuli.

egocentric The inability to see a situation from someone else's perspective. According to Piaget's theory of cognitive development, this takes place during the pre-operational stage, between two and six. He devised the 'three mountains' task', in which a child is asked to draw model mountains from the point of view of a movable doll, to show that children cannot imagine what things look like from other people's perspective.

environmental factors Most psychologists nowadays believe that people's development is shaped by a combination of genetic and environmental factors (the nature/nurture argument). Chief among the environmental factors are: family background, diet, exposure to disease, educational opportunities and social milieu. All can have a significant impact on a child's development, although it is also clear that someone brought up in an imperfect environment can develop normally and lead a happy and fulfilling life.

epistemology The study of the theoretical foundations of knowledge. It is mainly concerned with finding out what knowledge is and how it is acquired, and exploring how it relates to major life issues, such as the concept of truth.

hypothetical Assumed or theoretical, not proven. A hypothetical scenario is one that assumes certain unproven factors, which may (or may not) be proven correct through scientific observation. Most scientific theories start off as hypotheses that are over time proven true.

internalization In developmental psychology, the way a child acquires knowledge through social interaction with another person (usually a parent). First the child experiences a situation with another person, then re-experiences the situation within him/herself, until it becomes part of the child's body of knowledge. This process is thought to apply to functions such as language, memory and abstract thought.

methodology A set of theories, rules and procedures applied to a particular field of study or other endeavour. What is appropriate in one discipline may not be in another.

moral development The process through which children learn the difference between right and wrong. Jean Piaget believed that children initially judge good and bad by the consequences of people's actions (such as, did anyone get hurt? Was anything broken?), which then changes to a consideration of people's intentions (e.g. did they mean to hurt someone/break something?). Kohlberg went further and divided moral development into six stages, the highest of which only 10 per cent of adults achieve.

neuroscience The study of the nervous system, including the brain functions and how they relate to human behaviour. Ultimately the task of neuroscientists is to discover the functions of all parts of the brain, what mental processes they perform and how they are affected by external stimuli. Once a branch of biology, it is now regarded as an interdisciplinary science which covers several other disciplines, such as psychology, medicine and computer science.

psychoanalyst Someone who treats emotional disorders using the techniques of psychoanalytic theory that were developed by Sigmund Freud in the 1890s. Training involves four years' study, during which time the students themselves are obliged to undergo analysis.

schema A preconceived block of knowledge that helps us cope with unknown aspects of the world. At its best, it means we don't have to learn everything from scratch, such as how to drive a vehicle; we simply apply our 'driving schema' to any vehicle. At its worst, it means we presume knowledge we don't have and make prejudiced judgments, such as not stopping in the street to talk to people because we assume they are begging.

stereotypical Characterized by stereotypes; a way of thinking which involves stereotypes. Stereotypes are generalizations that are applied to a group of people without any consideration of individual variations. Thus, the idea that Jewish people are only interested in making money is a stereotypical view that doesn't allow for the fact that many Jewish people couldn't care less about making money.

surrogate A person or thing that acts as a substitute for someone or something else. The term is often applied to a woman or man who takes the place of a child's mother or father.

PIAGET'S STAGES
the 30-second theory

3-SECOND PSYCHE
Children are little scientists constructing their own understanding of the world, and their mistakes are the best indicators of how they think.

3-MINUTE ANALYSIS
Piaget was hugely influential, but his ideas have been heavily criticized. One major criticism is that he ignored the role of social factors in the development of knowledge. Another is that he did not use standardized methods – he started by asking children the same set of questions, but then tailored later questions according to the answers they gave. Furthermore, he did not use statistics to analyze his results, and did not account for individual differences.

As an epistemologist (someone who studies the nature of knowledge), Piaget was interested in how knowledge develops in humans, and regarded intelligence as the means by which we adapt to the environment. He believed that a child's understanding of reality is constructed through continuous interaction with the world, and that knowledge is organized into *schemas* – the basic building blocks of intelligent behaviour – which become increasingly complex as the child grows. Piaget suggested that knowledge develops in stages. In the *sensori-motor* stage (0–2 years), the child 'thinks' by perceiving objects and acting upon them. Towards the end of this stage, the child will search for hidden objects – 'out of sight' is no longer 'out of mind'. The *pre-operational* stage (2–7 years) is defined largely by the development and use of mental images, symbols and language. The child is egocentric, or self-centred, and cannot understand that others might see things differently. During the *concrete operational* stage (7–11 years), the child becomes less self-centred and can think logically, but still needs to manipulate objects in order to do so. The *formal operational* stage (11–15 years) is marked by the ability to manipulate ideas and to think hypothetically about situations not yet experienced.

RELATED THEORIES
See also
VYGOTSKY'S ZONE
Page 34
KOHLBERG'S MORAL STAGES
Page 42

3-SECOND BIOGRAPHY
JEAN PIAGET
1896–1980

30-SECOND TEXT
Moheb Costandi

Piaget believed that the child's mind develops, brick by brick, through discrete stages.

VYGOTSKY'S ZONE
the 30-second theory

3-SECOND PSYCHE
Children are young apprentices, acquiring knowledge and new skills through guided collaboration with those who already possess them.

3-MINUTE ANALYSIS
Despite dying at the age of 37, Vygotsky made a significant contribution to psychology, and his ideas are particularly relevant to education. As well as questioning the validity of standardized testing, he showed how teachers can support pupils' intellectual development by means of interactions and instructions structured around the tasks they can perform independently. In so doing, the teacher provides a 'scaffold', or context, within which the pupil can exercise her existing knowledge to solve the problem at hand.

For Vygotsky, our ability to think and reason is largely the product of a social process. Young children can do very little by or for themselves, and learn instead by interacting with others. By taking part in social activities with 'expert' tutors or instructors, such as parents and teachers, they move towards independence and self-sufficiency. This involves a gradual transformation of their intellectual abilities: the problem-solving process initially takes place within the social setting, but becomes 'internalized' as the child follows by example. Consider pointing – at first, it is little more than an indicatory gesture, the baby's failed attempt at grasping something beyond her reach. When the mother sees her baby pointing, she helps out, and may point to the object herself. As a result, the baby learns to point to an object out of her reach, then gazes at her mother. The pointing gesture is intended as a signal to the mother that she wants the object she is pointing to. Vygotsky's 'zone of proximal development' refers to the gap between the child's actual and potential development, or what she has already mastered and what she can do under the guidance of an adult. Accordingly, IQ tests cannot provide a measure of the child's true capabilities, because they only indicate what she can do unassisted.

RELATED THEORIES
See also
PIAGET'S STAGES
Page 32
KOHLBERG'S MORAL STAGES
Page 42

3-SECOND BIOGRAPHY
LEV VYGOTSKY
1896–1934

30-SECOND TEXT
Moheb Costandi

Vygotsky pointed out that children don't learn in a social vacuum, but by interacting with, and observing, others.

BIRTH ORDER

the 30-second theory

The idea that birth order can

have a lasting influence on personality and behaviour was first suggested by the influential psychologist Alfred Adler in the 1930s. Adler argued that the eldest child is socially dominant and intellectual, but tends to seek approval from others because he is no longer the centre of attention following the birth of a sibling; that the middle child, being sandwiched between older and younger siblings, is competitive and diplomatic; and that the youngest child tends to be selfish and demanding, since he is used to being provided for. Adler also stated, however, that although birth order is a contributory factor, it is environmental conditions, such as socioeconomic circumstances, that ultimately shape personality. There is no doubt that parents treat their first and second siblings differently – they can devote more time, attention and resources to, and tend to be more protective of, their first child. With the birth of a sibling, the firstborn loses his status as the only child, and the parents divide their time between the two. This differential treatment could plausibly affect the children's personalities, but it is impossible to establish exactly how, because its effects cannot be isolated from those of other factors such as sex, the age gap between siblings and socioeconomic status.

3-SECOND PSYCHE
A person's rank by age among their siblings affects their psychological development and personality.

3-MINUTE ANALYSIS
Although the idea that birth order affects personality is very popular, it has proved to be highly controversial, because there is very little scientific evidence to support it. Many of the studies investigating birth order effects do not take the confounding variables into account. Recent research lends some credence to the idea, however, with one 2009 study showing that lower birth rank has a negative, albeit small, effect on IQ.

RELATED THEORIES
See also
PIAGET'S STAGES
Page 32
KOHLBERG'S MORAL STAGES
Page 42

3-SECOND BIOGRAPHY
ALFRED ADLER
1870–1937

30-SECOND TEXT
Moheb Costandi

If you're the first born, you get your parents' undivided attention – but remember, they've never done this before!

1896
Born, Neuchâtel,
Switzerland

1921
Research Director at
Rousseau Institute,
Geneva

1923
Marries Valentine
Châtenay

1925
Professor of Psychology,
University of Neuchâtel

1929
Professor of
Experimental Psychology,
University of Geneva

1952
Publishes *The Origin of
Intelligence in Children*

1955
Establishes the
International Centre for
Genetic Epistemology

1980
Dies in Geneva,
Switzerland

JEAN PIAGET

According to Jean Piaget,

children start thinking like an adult between the ages of 11 and 15. No surprise then that the start of his own adult consciousness can be traced back to events that happened when he was around that age. Aged 10 or 11 (he was precocious), the young Piaget wrote a one-page article about an albino pigeon he had spotted in his home town of Neuchâtel in Switzerland. The piece was published by a natural history journal, and Piaget's first career was launched. Tutored by the head of the natural history museum, he became an expert on molluscs and, when his mentor died a few years later, wrote articles for various scientific journals – the editors of which all assumed he was an adult. Aged 21, he was awarded a doctoral degree from Neuchâtel University for his study of molluscs.

But it was while studying psychology at the Sorbonne in Paris that Piaget stumbled across the subject that would earn him global recognition. After meeting Théodore Simon, one of the creators of the Binet–Simon intelligence test, he was asked to apply the system to children at a school in Paris where Alfred Binet was conducting research. Although critical of the rigid nature of the tests, Piaget became fascinated by why children consistently got certain questions wrong. As he questioned the children, he not only discovered the subject he would study for the rest of his life – how knowledge develops – but also the methodology: one-to-one interviews with his subjects.

Piaget would go on to write more than fifty books and hundreds of articles, mostly about child development, although he always maintained that he was not a child psychologist but a genetic epistemologist, as his true interest was in the development of knowledge. His favourite subjects were his three children, who were the subjects for much of his early work, up to and well beyond the age of 12.

HARLOW'S MONKEYS

the 30-second theory

Harry Harlow was interested in the formation of the bond between mother and child, and tried to assess the relative importance of the child's need for food and its need for comfort. In a set of famous, but unethical, experiments, he separated newborn rhesus monkeys from their biological mothers and raised them in cages with 'surrogate' mothers. The infant monkeys were made to choose between two different surrogates – one was made of wire and had a bottle of milk attached to it, while the other was made of soft and cuddly towelling but did not have a bottle. Harlow found that the infants spent most of their time clinging to the cloth mother, even though 'she' provided no nourishment. In another experiment, he placed the infants into cages containing only one of the two surrogates. Those caged in with a cloth mother felt secure enough to explore their new environment, and would run back and cling to 'her' when frightened by a loud noise. By contrast, the infants placed with the wire surrogate did not explore their cage and, when frightened, would either freeze and cower, or run around the cage aimlessly.

RELATED THEORIES
See also
WATSON'S BEHAVIOURISM
Page 16

3-SECOND PSYCHE
Newborn monkeys need warmth, contact and comfort at least as much as they need food and water, and this probably applies to human infants, too.

3-MINUTE ANALYSIS
Harlow showed that baby monkeys have an unlearned need for contact comfort that is as basic as the need for food. By doing so, he challenged the 'cupboard love' attachment theories popular with behaviourists and psychoanalysts, which stated that the infant bonds with its mother because she can satisfy its instinctive need for nourishment. He also argued that fathers can make equally good care-givers as mothers, a revolutionary idea at the time.

3-SECOND BIOGRAPHY
HARRY HARLOW
1905–1981

30-SECOND TEXT
Moheb Costandi

Harlow's research into infant monkeys found that babies don't cuddle mothers as a bribe for milk, they really do like the affection.

KOHLBERG'S MORAL STAGES

the 30-second theory

30-SECOND PSYCHE
A child's sense of morality develops in a stereotypical way and is based on the fundamental principle of justice.

3-MINUTE ANALYSIS
Kohlberg found that the answers given by children of different nationalities and ages are reasonably consistent with regard to his stages of moral development. Some psychologists have argued that most children are unfamiliar with the moral dilemmas used, and might provide more mature answers to problems that are more relevant to them. Others point out that the emphasis on justice makes Kohlberg's theory inherently sexist, because qualities that traditionally define female 'goodness', such as caring for others, are lower on his scale.

Lawrence Kohlberg studied moral development by presenting children with moral dilemmas involving a conflict between two or more moral principles. He classified his participants according to their level of moral development on the basis of the reasoning behind the answers they gave. Kohlberg identified three levels of moral development, each consisting of two stages. At stage 1, the child's sense of what is right and wrong is determined by what is punishable and what is not, and at stage 2 by what others want and what brings reward. At stage 3, good behaviour is characterized by whatever pleases and helps others, and at stage 4 by showing respect for authority. At stage 5, children understand that, although rules should normally be followed, they are sometimes superseded by the rights of the individual. At stage 6, the highest level, actions are determined by self-chosen ethical principles – such as justice, equality and respect for human dignity – which are established through reflection. These principles are abstract and universal, and full moral responsibility can only be attained by acting in accordance with them. Kohlberg believed that only about 10 per cent of adults reach this level of moral reasoning, and later concluded that stage 6 may not be a separate stage after all.

RELATED THEORIES
See also
PIAGET'S STAGES
Page 32

3-SECOND BIOGRAPHY
LAWRENCE KOHLBERG
1927–1987

30-SECOND TEXT
Moheb Costandi

'Dad, it's not fair that you're telling me off for bad behaviour now – I've only reached Kohlberg's fifth stage of morality'.

NEUROPLASTICITY

the 30-second theory

Plastic means flexible.

Neuroplasticity is the collection of ways in which the brain changes in response to what we do and experience. If you believe the mind is the activity of the brain, then every change in your mind must, logically, entail changes in your brain. Considered this way, evidence of neuroplasticity should be expected. What really surprises neuroscientists is the extent to which the brain can change in response to injuries or new challenges. Supposedly 'visual' areas of the brain are recruited by the sense of touch in the blind, or – as demonstrated by Alvaro Pascual-Leone – even in sighted people who live with a blindfold on for five days. This reorganization according to a person's activities (such as seeing or touching) seems to be a general principle of brain development. This principle operates throughout the lifetime, not just in childhood. So, to take a famous example, a part of the brain involved in navigation has been shown to be larger in London cab drivers, who spend their adult lives finding their way around the city. The concept of neuroplasticity is tied to the idea that we can change how we think, and our abilities, throughout our lifetime and that keeping mentally active can help us to remain flexible and alert in older age.

3-SECOND PSYCHE
What you do and think can change the structure of your brain.

3-MINUTE ANALYSIS
One reason neuroplasticity is currently much discussed is that it contradicts the idea that the mind is a static, computer-like, information-processing machine. Another might be that people find it surprising because, even though it is orthodoxy that the mind is based on the brain, we still don't, in our hearts, believe that all our thoughts and feelings are due to a lump of meat between our ears.

RELATED THEORIES
See also
PAVLOV'S DOGS
Page 134

3-SECOND BIOGRAPHY
ALVARO PASCUAL-LEONE
1961–

30-SECOND TEXT
Tom Stafford

Brains can be flexible – research into blind people has shown that their other senses often commandeer the redundant visual parts of their brains.

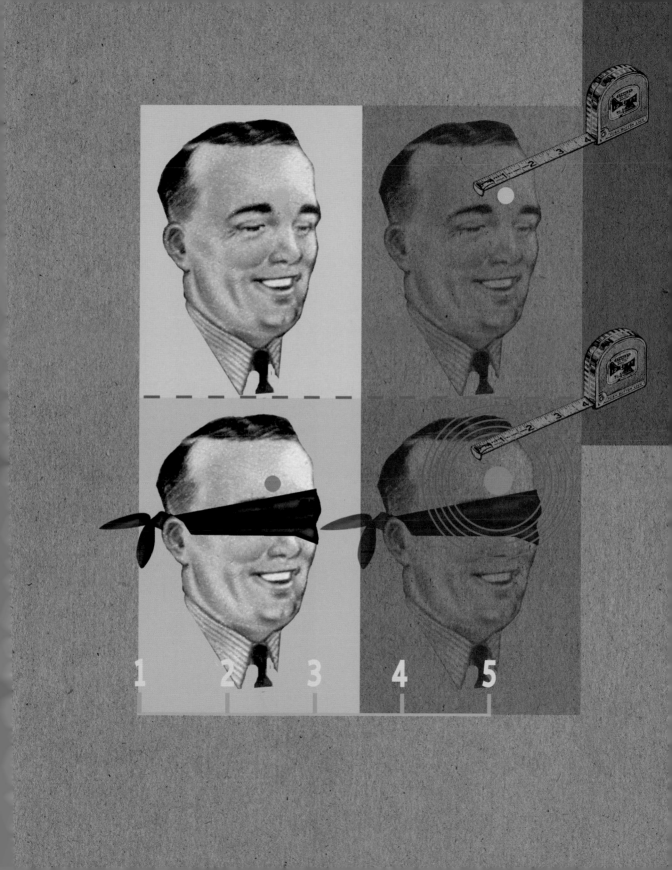

DECISION MAKING & EMOTIONS

DECISION MAKING & EMOTIONS
GLOSSARY

amygdala Part of the brain that controls fear, aggression and emotional memory. There are two amygdalae that share this role, one on either side of the brain, buried deep in the temporal lobes. Studies have shown that when the amygdalae of aggressive animals are damaged, they become docile and even timid.

behavioural economics A branch of economics which looks at the factors that influence people's financial decisions. Drawing on psychology, behavioural economics shows that, far from the picture of rational 'economic man' painted by classical economics, people frequently base their decisions on impulse, prejudice and intuition. Psychological impulses range from altruism to outright self-sabotage.

cold state In an unaroused condition, as opposed to 'hot state', which is when our appetites are aroused. The term has its origins in the so-called hot-cold empathy gaps described by US psychologist George Loewenstein and developed by Loran Nordgren and others. Loewenstein found that people in an unaroused ('cold') state failed to anticipate their behaviour when aroused (or 'hot'). He used the example of young men failing to predict that, in the heat of the moment, they would be tempted to have sex without a condom, leading to risk-taking sexual behaviour.

expected utility This is a way of working out people's betting preferences taking into account all factors, including risk aversion and personal preference. This differs from expected value, which is purely focused on the financial gain expected from a gamble. Expected utility explains why people don't always make the decision that, rationally, you might expect them to.

frontal lobes The front part of the brain, that is involved with motor skills, moral judgments, language, decision making and long-term memory.

hippocampus Part of the brain that is responsible for long-term memory, located in the frontal lobes.

hot state In an aroused condition, as opposed to 'cold state'.

innate An essential part of something or someone, possibly existing since birth. From the Latin *innatus*, meaning to be born in.

intuition Knowledge gained through instinct, rather than a rational process. From the Latin *intuito*, meaning 'to look at'.

neurologist A doctor who specializes in treating the nervous system, including the brain. Diagnosis includes the physical condition of the brain, physical functions affected by the brain, such as balance and motor skills, and cognitive abilities, such as memory and speech. Treatment includes referral to a physiotherapist, prescribing drugs and/or surgery.

physiological Relating to the normal functioning of a body. A physiological reaction is a response usually triggered by the brain. There is ongoing debate about what stage the conscious brain engages, and whether emotions trigger the reaction or vice versa. The classic example given in the James–Lange theory of emotion is that of a person coming across a bear in the woods. Their physiological reaction is to tremble and then run. According to James–Lange, however, fear is triggered by the physiological reaction, which the brain recognizes as a symptom of fear, rather than vice versa.

prefrontal cortex The foremost part of the brain, located in the anterior (front) region of the frontal lobes. It is responsible for expressing personality, moral judgments and controlling sexual impulses.

restraint bias The tendency for people to be unduly optimistic about their ability to control their behaviour when aroused. The term originates in the theory of hot-cold empathy gaps described by US psychologist George Loewenstein and developed by Loran Nordgren and others.

schizophrenia A psychiatric diagnosis associated with abnormalities in several of the brain's neurotransmitters. Typically, the condition is marked by a distorted view of reality, an inability to function socially, withdrawal from society, hearing voices and delusions of grandeur. Sub-categories include: paranoid, disorganized, catatonic, undifferentiated and residual schizophrenia.

stimulus Something that stimulates a response. In certain instances, the strength of a psychological stimulus may elicit an uncontrolled physical response, such as nervous twitches or spasms.

systematic Relating to the entire system, in this case the brain. A systematic problem is one that requires the whole system to be treated for the problem to be eradicated.

EKMAN'S
UNIVERSAL
EMOTIONS

the 30-second theory

The idea that human expressions are universal dates back to Darwin and was popularized by Paul Ekman in the 1970s. Ekman argues that muscle movements in the face are the building blocks of facial expressions, and that the relationship between these movements and emotions is universal. He showed photos of faces expressing various emotions to people from different parts of the world, including North and South America, Japan, and the Fore peoples of the Papua New Guinea highlands, and found that they all identified the same faces with the same emotional words. He also filmed the facial expressions of US and Japanese students as they watched movies, and observed the same expressions in both. He took these results as evidence that the expression of emotions is constant across cultures, and suggested that this apparent universality is due to evolution, innate brain mechanisms or common developmental processes. Ekman used his findings to devise the Facial Action Coding System (FACS), a comprehensive index of facial expressions. He applied the FACS to the study of how expressions change in people with psychiatric disorders, and argued that people with depression and schizophrenia cannot recognize specific emotions. Today, the FACS is still the most commonly used method for categorizing facial expressions.

RELATED THEORY
See also
EVOLUTIONARY PSYCHOLOGY
Page 24

3-SECOND BIOGRAPHY
PAUL EKMAN
1934–

30-SECOND TEXT
Moheb Costandi

3-SECOND PSYCHE
People from different cultures use the same facial expressions to convey emotions, such as anger, fear, disgust, sadness and surprise.

3-MINUTE ANALYSIS
Since Ekman's work, it has generally been accepted that facial expressions are the universal language of emotions. However, a 2009 study showed that Western Europeans and Asians use a different strategy to decode facial expressions, and that the strategy employed by Asians cannot reliably distinguish between FACS-coded expressions of fear and disgust – thus suggesting that the expressions of emotions are not universal after all.

Ekman's Facial Action Coding System categorizes and documents every conceivable human facial expression according to which muscles or 'action units' are tensed at any given time.

10	·7893	1·775	3·162	4·938	7·113
20	1.116	2·511	4·472	6·983	10·06
30	1·367	3·076	5·477	8·553	12·32
40	1·578	3·557	6·324	9·876	14·22
50	1·764	3·971	7·071	11·04	15·90
60	1·933	4·350	7·746	12·09	17·42
70	2·88	4·698	8·366	13·06	18·82
80	2·232	5·023	8·944	13·96	20·12
90	2·367	5·327	9·486	14·81	21·34
100	2·496	5·61	10·00	15·61	22·49
110	2·617	5·890	10·48	16·37	23·59
120	2·734	6·151	10·	17·10	24·64
130	2·845	6·402	11·40	17·80	25·64
140	2·953	6·644	11·83	18·47	26·61
150	3·056	6·877	12·24	19·12	27·55
160	3·157	7·103	12·64	19·75	28·45
170	3·254	7·322	13·03	20·36	29·33
180	3·348	7·534	13·41	20·95	30·18
190	3·440	7·741	13·78	21·52	31·00
200		7·942	14·14	22·08	31·81
210	3·616	8·138		·62	32·59
220	3·702	8·329	14·83	23·16	33·36
230	3·785	8·516	15·16	23·68	34·11
240	3·866	8·699	15·49	24·19	34·84
250	3·946	8·879	15·81	·69	35·56
260	4·024	9·055	16·12	·17	36·27
270	4·101	9·209	16·43	·65	36·96
280	4·176	9·397	16·73	·13	37·64
290	4·250	9·563	17·02	·59	38·30
300	4·323	9·726	17·32	·04	38·96
310	4·394	9·888	17·60	·8	39·60
320	4·464	10·04	17·88	·93	40·24

FESTINGER'S BORING TASK

the 30-second theory

If you believe one thing, yet do or say another, what happens psychologically? In the absence of any external justification for the anomalous behaviour, the contradiction is resolved by altering your original belief. The American psychologist Leon Festinger showed this with James Carlsmith in a classic study in 1959, known as 'the boring task'. Having performed an hour-long monotonous task involving pegs on a board, students were paid either one dollar or twenty dollars to convince another person that the task was fun and interesting. Afterwards, the students were asked by a researcher what they really thought of the boring task: those paid just one dollar said that they had found the task enjoyable whereas the students paid twenty dollars said that it was in truth terribly dull. Festinger's interpretation was that the students' belief that the task was dull clashed with the fact that they'd just told someone else it was fun, thus causing uncomfortable 'cognitive dissonance'. For the students who had been paid twenty dollars, this contradiction was easily resolved – they'd been paid a fair sum and that's why they'd lied. For the students who had been paid just one dollar, however, the contradiction was more easily resolved by altering their original belief.

RELATED THEORIES
See also
WASON'S CONFIRMATION BIAS
Page 60
THE LAKE WOBEGON EFFECT
Page 90

3-SECOND BIOGRAPHIES
LOUISA EGAN
1983–

LEON FESTINGER
1919–1989

30-SECOND TEXT
Christian Jarrett

3-SECOND PSYCHE
Whenever a pair of incompatible beliefs or decisions collide in our minds, it provokes a kind of mental discomfort known as 'cognitive dissonance'.

3-MINUTE ANALYSIS
It's not just us humans who experience cognitive dissonance – monkeys do, too. Louisa Egan and her colleagues at Yale University showed this in a 2007 study in which they offered capuchin monkeys the choice between pairs of differently coloured, yet equally appealing sweets. After turning down a given colour in one pair, a monkey made subsequent choices that showed it had devalued that rejected colour in its mind, thereby justifying the earlier arbitrary preference.

Just tell yourself that putting pegs in a board all day is a whole lot of fun and you'll start to believe it.

THE JAMES–LANGE THEORY OF EMOTION

the 30-second theory

The letter lands with a soft thud on the doormat. You rip open the envelope, scan the text and there it is, the crucial line announcing you've got the job. Joy rises up causing a huge smile to spread across your face. Wait a minute. According to the James–Lange theory of emotion – proposed independently by the great US psychologist William James and the Danish physiologist Carl Lange – this description has it back to front. James and Lange argued that a stimulus, in this case the good news, triggers a physiological reaction, such as a racing heartbeat and the spread of a smile, and it is these bodily and facial changes that cause the emotion, in this case joy. Writing in the late nineteenth century James gave the example of a confrontation with a bear. We don't become frightened, tremble and then run, he argued. Rather, we tremble and run, and it's those bodily changes that cause us to feel frightened. The James–Lange theory was challenged in the early twentieth century by the physiologist Walter Cannon. He conducted grisly experiments showing that dogs still exhibited emotions even after he'd severed their spinal cords thereby preventing bodily feedback from reaching their brains.

If a bear comes charging towards you, keep smiling and you won't feel frightened at all. And who knows, maybe the bear will smile back.

1842
Born, New York City

1860
Studies painting

1865
Travels up the Amazon

1869
M.D. from Harvard

1872
Teaches anatomy and physiology at Harvard

1875
Teaches psychology at Harvard

1878
Marries Alice Howe Gibbens

1879
Teaches philosophy at Harvard

1890
Publishes *The Principles of Psychology*

1907
Resigns from Harvard

1910
Dies, Chocorua, New Hampshire

WILLIAM JAMES

Genius, it seems, runs in the family. And there are few families that demonstrate this better than the Jameses of New York. Not only was the patriarch of the family, Henry James Sen., a wealthy and respected theologian in his own right, but he was the father of three children who would in turn go on to achieve recognition in their own fields: the writer Henry James, the diarist Alice James and the psychologist William James.

It can't have been easy being a James progeny, however, as all five of Henry James Sen.'s children suffered variously from depression and/or miscellaneous physical ailments. Their upbringing, although privileged, was unsettling – travelling frequently between the United States and Europe – and seems to have affected the famous sons in parallel ways. While Henry started studying law at Harvard before switching to literature, William studied painting before switching to medicine and then teaching psychology at Harvard. Similarly, while Henry pioneered the use of the unreliable narrator and interior monologues in fiction, William, as well as being credited for the concept of 'stream of consciousness', is also known for his pragmatic theory of truth, in which he examined the nature of truth. One thing both brothers seemed certain of is that nothing is certain.

Like his brother, William was a prolific writer, but it was the publication of *The Principles of Psychology*, which took some twelve years to complete, that confirmed him as the 'father of American psychology'. The 1200-page tome and its condensed version *Psychology: The Briefer Course* (known respectively as *The James* and *The Jimmy*) soon became the standard reference for students of the subject. William himself was less enamoured with his creation, describing it as a 'loathsome, distended, tumefied, bloated, dropsical mass, testifying to nothing but two facts: first, that there is no such thing as a science of psychology, and second, that WJ is an incapable'. Harsh words indeed. His truth, however, was not everyone's truth.

DAMASIO'S EMOTIONAL DECISION MAKING

the 30-second theory

In the late 1970s, American neurologist Antonio Damasio noticed something peculiar in several of his patients. When certain parts of their brains were damaged, people with otherwise normal brain function found it difficult to make decisions. For example, one of his patients spent half an hour deliberating on the best time for his next appointment, until Damasio finally just told him when to show up. Subsequent experiments convinced Damasio that the damaged areas in these patients' brains were responsible for connecting emotions with knowledge and logic. Since emotions are generally experienced somatically (physically), he called his explanation of decision making the somatic marker hypothesis. When patients with damaged prefrontal cortices were shown emotional images, such as mutilated bodies or people having sex, their heart rate and other vital signs did not increase, as they do in people with undamaged brains. Similarly, these patients could not master a simple gambling game, losing all their money when normal people saw how to profit from it. The somatic marker hypothesis says the prefrontal cortex stores knowledge about emotions – such as the negative feelings associated with losing money – that helps us to make good decisions. Good decisions aren't just logical, they're emotional, too.

3-SECOND PSYCHE
Do you make decisions using cool logic or hot emotions? Probably both.

3-MINUTE ANALYSIS
The specific brain area associated with the somatic marker hypothesis is the ventromedial prefrontal cortex, just behind and above your eyes. Aside from observing the impairments in his patients, Damasio reasoned that it makes sense for this region to be involved in decision making. It not only receives inputs from all our senses, but also connects with emotional centres of the brain in the hippocampus and amygdala – and it's a part of the frontal lobe, where reasoning occurs.

RELATED THEORIES
See also
EVOLUTIONARY PSYCHOLOGY
Page 24
EKMAN'S UNIVERSAL EMOTIONS
Page 50
KAHNEMAN & TVERSKY'S PROSPECT THEORY
Page 64

3-SECOND BIOGRAPHIES
ANTOINE BECHARA
1961–
ANTONIO DAMASIO
1944–

30-SECOND TEXT
Dave Munger

Try to make a cool, calm, considered decision, and it might be a poorer one than if you'd allowed your emotions to kick in.

WASON'S CONFIRMATION BIAS

the 30-second theory

3-SECOND PSYCHE
We seek out and pay particular attention to information that supports our existing beliefs.

3-MINUTE ANALYSIS
We read newspapers that espouse our own political views and pay more attention to adverts that champion our favourite brands. What happens when we're confronted with scientific evidence that directly contradicts our personal beliefs? A 2010 study by Towson University psychologist Geoffrey Munro found that such a situation leads many of us to conclude that the topic at hand, and other topics, too, are not amenable to scientific inquiry – what he called 'the scientific impotence excuse'.

Back in the 1960s, the British psychologist Peter Wason presented research participants with four cards, each with a letter on one side and a number on the other. Two of them showed a letter on their upper face, the other two showed a number, rather like this: B, E, 4, 8. The participants' task was to say which cards they'd need to turn over to test the statement: 'If a card has a "B" on one side, it always has a "4" on the other.' Most participants said they'd turn over the 'B' card, which is fair enough—anything other than a '4' on the other side would refute the statement. However, the majority of participants then mistakenly said they'd turn over the '4'. Doing so is pointless. The presence of a 'B' on the other side would support the statement, but not conclusively. The presence of any other letter would have no bearing on the statement. The other card the participants should have opted to turn over is the '8'. If this revealed a 'B', the statement would be falsified. Known as the 'Wason selection task', this and other research Wason conducted showed our strong 'confirmation bias' – the tendency to seek out evidence that supports our existing beliefs.

RELATED THEORIES
See also
FESTINGER'S BORING TASK
Page 52
JANIS' GROUPTHINK
Page 72

3-SECOND BIOGRAPHY
PETER WASON
1924–2003

30-SECOND TEXT
Christian Jarrett

From voting to shopping, to improve your decision making try considering the reasons against, as well as the reasons for, your current favourite.

BAUMEISTER'S EGO DEPLETION

the 30-second theory

All fresh and crumbly, a biscuit sits on a plate under your nose. Can you resist it? It depends on what you've been up to earlier in the day. Research conducted over the last two decades by US psychologist Roy Baumeister has shown that willpower is a finite resource – straining to control yourself in one situation will leave you easily swayed later on. For example, in one classic study Baumeister instructed participants to sit in a room on their own, to resist the plate of chocolate biscuits and instead eat two or three of the radishes that were also available. Afterwards these abstemious participants gave up far earlier on an impossible puzzle than did other students who had been allowed to eat the biscuits. Bizarrely, a recent study showed that we can become 'ego-depleted' – Baumeister's term for when we're willpower-fatigued – merely by imagining the turmoil of another person forced to exercise self-restraint. The good news is there's evidence that, rather like a muscle, it's possible to build up our willpower through practice. Resist that biscuit today and, who knows, maybe it will be easier tomorrow.

RELATED THEORIES
See also
FESTINGER'S BORING TASK
Page 52
KAHNEMAN & TVERSKY'S
PROSPECT THEORY
Page 64

3-SECOND BIOGRAPHY
ROY BAUMEISTER
1953–

3-SECOND TEXT
Christian Jarrett

3-SECOND PSYCHE
Like the fuel in your car, willpower is a finite resource – using it up in one situation will leave you vulnerable to temptation in another.

3-MINUTE ANALYSIS
According to Northwestern University psychologist Loran Nordgren and his collaborators, one of the reasons we often leave ourselves open to temptation is that when we're satiated – what they call a cold state – we underestimate the strength of our desires when we're in a hot state (hungry, tired or lustful). They call this the 'restraint' bias.

If you've just eaten, you might be able to resist those chocolate biscuits, but don't underestimate their appeal once you're hungry again.

KAHNEMAN & TVERSKY'S PROSPECT THEORY

the 30-second theory

3-SECOND PSYCHE
Our calculations involving risk are biased depending on whether we stand to gain or lose.

3-MINUTE ANALYSIS
Prospect theory was part of the work that won Daniel Kahneman a Nobel Prize in Economics, and is foundational to the area known as 'behavioural economics', which seeks to uncover descriptions of the way we actually behave in defiance of supposedly rational behaviour. Because any gamble can result in a loss or a gain depending on what you assume the status quo is, an important consequence of prospect theory is that you can change how people feel about a bet by changing whether you describe it as a chance of a loss or a gain.

There is a rational way to do calculations that involve risks. If you have a choice between a 100 per cent chance of losing $15 and a 5 per cent chance of losing $400, you could multiply 15 by 1.00 and 400 by 0.05 and select the choice with the lowest result. This is known as calculating 'expected utility'. However, you probably don't use this method – when asked to make choices involving risks you probably use intuition. Daniel Kahneman and Amos Tversky developed prospect theory to describe such intuitions. A key aspect of their theory is that we think about risks of losing differently from the way we consider risks of winning. In the example above, the second choice has the lower expected utility ($400 x 0.05 = $20, in other words an 'expected' loss of $20, compared with $15 in the first choice) – but many people feel intuitively that they would prefer the second choice. Prospect theory describes this as being 'risk seeking for losses'. You will gamble on a big loss to avoid a dead cert small loss. The reverse is where you prefer a small certain gain to a gamble over a potentially much larger gain. Prospect theory describes this as being 'risk averse for gains'.

RELATED THEORIES
See also
THE COGNITIVE REVOLUTION
Page 22

DAMASIO'S EMOTIONAL
DECISION MAKING
Page 58

WASON'S CONFIRMATION BIAS
Page 60

3-SECOND BIOGRAPHIES
DANIEL KAHNEMAN
1934–

AMOS TVERSKY
1937–1996

30-SECOND TEXT
Tom Stafford

Losses pack about twice the emotional punch of gains of the same size.

SOCIAL PSYCHOLOGY

dehumanize A process whereby a person or a group of people is regarded as subhuman and therefore not deserving of the same rights accorded to other people. The process is usually triggered by a difference in skin colour, religion or intelligence. The classic example is the treatment of Jews by the Nazis, but more recent examples include the relationship between Tutsis and Hutus in Rwanda and between the Serbs and other groups in the former Yugoslavia.

group polarization The tendency of a group of like-minded people to adopt views that are more extreme than they would be expected to adopt as individuals. This happens when the group is highly energized, dissent is suppressed, and events appear to take on a life of their own. The result of this group dynamic can affect the decision of juries and lead to extreme action, such as mob lynchings.

hypothesis A theoretical explanation of a phenomenon, often predicting the outcome given a certain set of circumstances. Most scientific theories start off as hypotheses and, once they are proved, become theories.

individuality The sum of the characteristics of a person or thing that distinguishes them from others in the same group. Societies can be characterized as individualistic or collective, with most Western countries placing greater emphasis on individuality, while Asian countries encourage collectivism.

intergroup Taking place between two or more social groups. Intergroup relations play an important part in understanding social conflict, such as in black-Latino neighbourhoods in the United States. How people behave within a group can differ significantly from how they behave as individuals outside the group.

outgroup A group which is not part of one's own social grouping. An ingroup is a group of which one is either a member, or of which one aspires to be a member. All other groups are outgroups and are usually regarded with varying degrees of disdain or suspicion. The concept comes from social identity theory, which was developed by the sociologist Henri Tajfel and others in the 1970s to explain the origins of racial prejudice.

pathological Literally, something relating to pathology, or the study of disease. In psychology, it refers to behaviour caused by or indicating mental illness. Colloquially, it usually refers to behaviour that is considered excessive or well beyond the norm.

personality profile Summary of a person's personality usually conducted through some form of psychological testing. The results are matched to certain established types that are intended to predict a person's behaviour.

prototypical Relating to a prototype, or something that is most representative of a certain category. Thus, a hammer might be a prototypical tool. Other objects within that category can then be arranged according to their relationship to the prototype, for example, a screwdriver is smaller and lighter.

schizophrenia A psychiatric diagnosis associated with abnormalities in several of the brain's neurotransmitters. Typically, the condition is marked by a distorted view of reality, an inability to function socially, withdrawal from society, hearing voices and delusions of grandeur. Sub-categories include: paranoid, disorganized, catatonic, undifferentiated and residual schizophrenia.

self-esteem How people regard themselves. Someone with good self-esteem has a high sense of their own worth, whereas someone with poor self-esteem has a low sense of their own worth. Self-esteem has powerful impact on a person's behaviour.

social identity The ways in which a person categorizes themselves and others. There are four main strands: self-identity (a person's religious belief, their job), group identity (following a football team, joining a political party), comparison (comparing themselves with other groups), and psychological distinctiveness (their personal characteristics). A combination of these form a person's social identity. The theory was developed by Henri Tajfel in the 1970s.

systemic Being part of a larger system, rather than an isolated occurrence. Systemic psychology considers that people develop partly through their individual consciousness and partly through communication with others, giving them contact with the wider 'system'. The theory is an offshoot of systems theory and was developed by Gregory Bateson in the 1970s.

THE BYSTANDER EFFECT

the 30-second theory

In the Kew Gardens district of New York in March 1964, bar manager Kitty Genovese was stabbed to death. Her demise was reportedly witnessed by thirty-eight apartment residents, none of whom did a thing to help. The tragedy caused a moral outcry in the local press and it inspired the psychologists John Darley and Bibb Latané to research a phenomenon that's come to be known as the 'bystander effect'. In their seminal 1968 paper, Darley and Latané tricked research participants into thinking that another participant in the room was having some kind of seizure. The key finding was that participants who thought they were on their own in the room with the 'victim' were far more likely to seek help, and to do so more quickly, than were participants seated in the room with three or four others. One explanation for the phenomenon is that the presence of other people reduces our own sense of responsibility for a situation.

RELATED THEORIES
See also
ZIMBARDO'S PRISON
Page 76
MILGRAM'S OBEDIENCE STUDY
Page 80
FUNDAMENTAL ATTRIBUTION ERROR
Page 94

3-SECOND PSYCHE
The more people present at a given situation, the less likely we are to intervene when someone is in need of help.

3-MINUTE ANALYSIS
When historian Joseph de May analyzed proceedings from the trial of Winston Moseley – Kitty Genovese's murderer – he found the story that thirty-eight witnesses did nothing was little more than a myth based on inaccurate newspaper reports of the time. In fact, Moseley's second fatal attack on Genovese took place in a stairwell out of view of all but one known witness. However, countless psychology studies have confirmed that the bystander effect is real.

3-SECOND BIOGRAPHIES
JOHN DARLEY
1938–

KITTY GENOVESE
1935–1964

BIBB LATANÉ
1937–

30-SECOND TEXT
Christian Jarrett

Don't walk on by. If we all assume that someone else will do something to help, then a tragedy could occur.

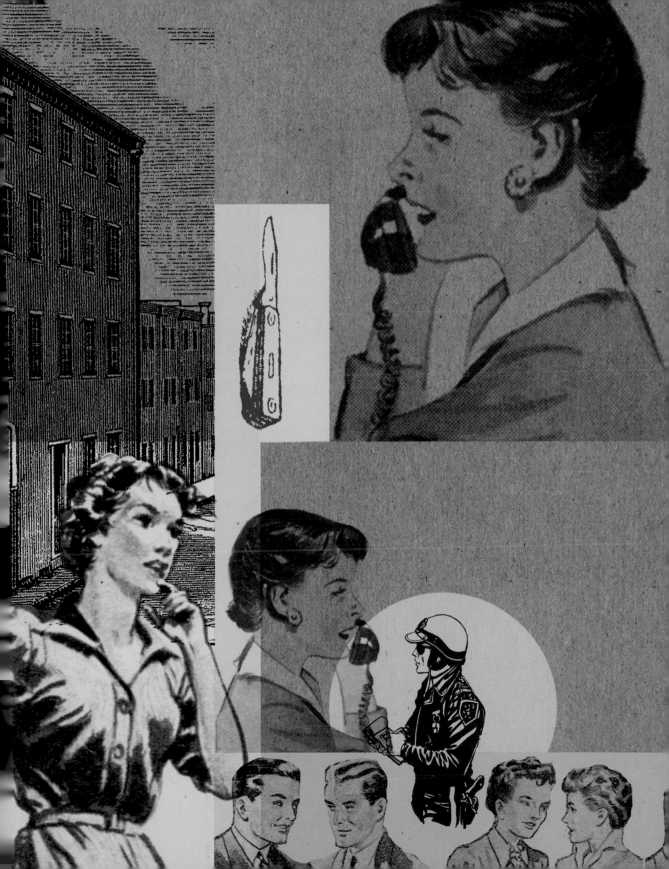

JANIS' GROUPTHINK

the 30-second theory

Experts and lay people alike used to think that groups make more conservative decisions than individuals. The mistaken reasoning was that groups come to decisions that reflect the average position of all group members, thereby diluting extremist views. A groundbreaking study by James Stoner in 1961, since replicated hundreds of times, showed that in fact groups make more polarized decisions than individuals. Whether it be in relation to financial risk-taking or political attitudes, group discussion accentuates any initial bias held by group members. In the early 1970s, Yale University psychologist Irving Janis argued that certain conditions can lead to a particularly extreme form of group polarization called 'groupthink', in which a dangerous illusion of consensus takes over. The preconditions for groupthink include members being close-knit and like-minded, a group leader who makes his or her own position known, and the group being shut off from other influences and opinions. Janis argued that groupthink was responsible for the catastrophic decision making that led to the Bay of Pigs Invasion and the United States' failure to anticipate Japan's attack on Pearl Harbor.

History shows that groups are capable of making terrible decisions, especially when they are cut off from dissenting opinions.

ALLPORT'S CONTACT HYPOTHESIS

the 30-second theory

Prejudice emerges at an early age. Young children show a preference for playing with other children of the same skin colour or with other kids who simply happen to be wearing similar clothes. In adulthood, in extreme cases, this instinct for prejudice can lead us to dehumanize those we consider to be outsiders. The antidote, according to the US psychologist Gordon Allport, is intergroup contact. The idea is that by coming into contact with 'others' we discover that they're human, too. Numerous studies, many of them conducted in known sectarian trouble spots such as Northern Ireland, have confirmed that people who have contact with outgroup members tend to have more positive attitudes towards members of that outgroup. For contact to be beneficial, an outsider must be seen as being representative of the group to which they belong. Contact also needs to be meaningful. When members of different social groups exchange intimacies they come to appreciate how much they have in common.

RELATED THEORIES
See also
WASON'S CONFIRMATION BIAS
Page 60
JANIS' GROUPTHINK
Page 72
ZIMBARDO'S PRISON
Page 76
FOLLOW THE LEADER
Page 84

3-SECOND BIOGRAPHY
GORDON ALLPORT
1897–1967

30-SECOND TEXT
Christian Jarrett

The humanity that we share overwhelms any superficial differences between races or other groups. Intergroup contact helps make this apparent.

ZIMBARDO'S PRISON

the 30-second theory

3-SECOND PSYCHE
A study of prison dynamics conducted in the early 1970s was abandoned when participants acting as guards began treating the mock prisoners with brutality.

3-MINUTE ANALYSIS
Zimbardo's Stanford prison experiment was the focus of renewed interest in 2004 when reports of prisoner abuse by US guards at the Abu Ghraib prison in Iraq first surfaced. In fact Zimbardo acted as an expert witness for the defence in the court martial of Sgt Ivan 'Chip' Frederick, where he argued that the prison environment, plus wider political and systemic circumstances, were largely to blame for the atrocities.

One California morning in 1971, twelve students were arrested by the local police and taken to a mock prison where they were shackled and clothed in knee-length smocks. The men had volunteered to take part in a psychological study of prison life. Another twelve students out of the seventy-five who volunteered were allocated to play the role of prison guards. The study, known today as the 'Stanford prison experiment', was scheduled to last two weeks but was abandoned after just six days. Philip Zimbardo, the psychologist in charge, says that he aborted because treatment of the prisoners by the guards had sunk to 'pornographic and degrading abuse', and also because of a visit by his future wife, Christina Maslach, a young psychologist who expressed horror at what was taking place. Some prisoners were extremely distressed and around a third of the guards were behaving in a sadistic fashion. Prestudy personality profiles of those participants who ended up acting as sadistic guards gave no clues as to what they were capable of – all were judged to be emotionally stable and law-abiding. Zimbardo says the study shows how certain situations and social roles can strip people of their individuality, prompting them to acts of sadism or submission.

RELATED THEORIES
See also
THE BYSTANDER EFFECT
Page 70
ALLPORT'S CONTACT HYPOTHESIS
Page 74
MILGRAM'S OBEDIENCE STUDY
Page 80
FOLLOW THE LEADER
Page 84
FUNDAMENTAL ATTRIBUTION ERROR
Page 94

3-SECOND BIOGRAPHY
PHILIP ZIMBARDO
1933–

30-SECOND TEXT
Christian Jarrett

According to Zimbardo, bad barrels, not bad apples, are the cause of many abuses.

1933
Born, New York

1954
Ph.D. at Harvard

1960
Assistant professor at
Yale University

1961
Marries Alexandra Menkin

1963
Assistant professor at Harvard

1963
Publishes 'Behavioural study
of Obedience'

1967
Professor at City University of
New York (CUNY)

1974
Publishes *Obedience to Authority*

1975
Obedience to Authority wins
National Book Award

1980
Distinguished Professor, CUNY

1984
Dies, New York

STANLEY MILGRAM

Few psychology experiments

have caught the public imagination as much as the obedience tests Stanley Milgram carried out in the 1960s. The so-called 'Milgram experiment' has featured in documentaries, movies, pop songs and, in France, formed the basis of a TV series in 2010. Yet Milgram didn't plan a career in psychology, and his application to study the subject was initially rejected. Milgram was born in the Bronx, New York, to ███sh parents – his Romanian mother had come to New York when she was four years old and his father had emigrated from Hungary after World War I. Because of his limited financial means, he took a B.A. in Political Science at Queens College, where tuition was free. He applied to study Social Psychology at Harvard, but was turned down on the basis that he had no background in the subject – having failed to take a single course in psychology at Queens. Undaunted, he spent the summer of 1954 accumulating psychology credits and was eventually accepted via Harvard's Office of Special Students.

Success came early with his obedience experiments, which were first published as 'Behavioural Study of Obedience' in the *Journal of Abnormal and Social Psychology* in 1963. Frustratingly, it wasn't just the test results that brought almost immediate worldwide attention, but the techniques Milgram used to achieve them, with critics accusing him of subjecting participants to excessive stress. His application to the American Psychological Association was delayed while his methods were investigated. After completing his Ph.D., at Harvard, he accepted the position of assistant professor at Yale University. Three years later he was invited back to Harvard as an assistant professor. In 1967 he took up a position as professor at City University of New York, where he would remain for the rest of his life. Although he was best known for his obedience experiments, Milgram also conducted influential experiments in the 'small world phenomenon' (or 'six degrees of separation') and the psychological effects of urban environments.

MILGRAM'S OBEDIENCE STUDY

the 30-second theory

Stanley Milgram wanted to

understand how ordinary people could take part in extraordinary cruelty. He was inspired by the terrible example of the Holocaust, in which ordinary citizens and soldiers collaborated in the evil schemes of the Nazis. In his experiments, volunteers took part in what they thought was a study of memory, giving electric shocks to a partner whenever he forgot things. In reality no shocks were given and the partner was an actor, who howled and protested as the volunteer delivered what he thought were more and more intense shocks. Would ordinary people deliver shocks of lethal voltage to an innocent man? When a scientist in a white coat stood in the corner of the room and merely reassured the volunteers with phrases such as 'the experiment requires that you continue', 65 per cent would deliver what they believed were lethal shocks. Milgram's study was actually a series of eighteen studies, which tested how different factors affected the likelihood that volunteers would obey an authority figure and deliver lethal shocks. He found that the remoteness of the victim, the authority of the person giving the orders and the presence of others in the same situation who obeyed, all increased the likelihood of someone complying with orders to kill.

3-SECOND PSYCHE
We're all capable of doing awful things to others if told to by someone in authority.

3-MINUTE ANALYSIS
When Milgram described his procedure in detail to a group of psychiatrists they predicted that only a 'pathological fringe' would obey the experimenter to the lethal end. Many who hear of Milgram's study protest they wouldn't obey, or that people today wouldn't behave in the same way (Milgram carried out his studies in the 1960s and 1970s). Unfortunately, the lesson Milgram teaches about the dangers of obedience to authority is as true today as it was when he carried out his classic studies.

RELATED THEORIES
See also
THE BYSTANDER EFFECT
Page 70
ZIMBARDO'S PRISON
Page 76

3-SECOND BIOGRAPHY
STANLEY MILGRAM
1933–1984

30-SECOND TEXT
Tom Stafford

Would you deliver a lethal electric shock to an innocent man just because an authority figure told you to? Research suggests that you probably would.

STEREOTYPE THREAT

the 30-second theory

A group of friends enjoy a throwing competition on a beach. As one of the girls curls back her arm ready to throw, niggling at her mind is an awareness that the boys in the group think girls can't throw. Their belief is of course a gross generalization and the girl is anxious that if her throw is weak it will only serve to reinforce the boys' sexist assumptions. Unfortunately, this anxiety undermines her performance – a self-fulfilling effect known as stereotype threat. The phenomenon of stereotype threat was christened by Claude Steele and Joshua Aronson in 1995 after they discovered that black participants performed worse at an intelligence test when it was described to them as a test of ability, rather than as an investigation of how people generally solve problems. Since then, stereotype threat has been documented in relation to other social contexts including gender and mental illness. For example, female chess players perform more poorly when they think they're up against a male opponent, and patients with schizophrenia have been found to behave more awkwardly when they think their diagnosis has been revealed to a social partner, even when it hasn't.

RELATED THEORIES
See also
ALLPORT'S CONTACT HYPOTHESIS
Page 74
FOLLOW THE LEADER
Page 84
FUNDAMENTAL ATTRIBUTION ERROR
Page 94

3-SECOND BIOGRAPHIES
JOSHUA ARONSON
1961–
CLAUDE STEELE
1946–

30-SECOND TEXT
Christian Jarrett

3-SECOND PSYCHE
Fearing that if we perform badly, other people will use that as evidence to reinforce their prejudices can cause us anxiety and make a poor performance more likely.

3-MINUTE ANALYSIS
Psychologist Geoff Cohen tested a possible buffer against stereotype threat. He asked black and white 12-year-old students to spend ten minutes, several times a year, writing about something they valued – such as family or music – an exercise known to reduce stress and fear of failure. The minority black pupils, at risk of stereotype threat, showed improved grades two years later whereas the majority white children did not; nor did a control group of both black and white pupils who wrote about their morning routine.

If you fear that your performance will be used to reinforce stereotypes about your sex, age or race, the situation could unfortunately become self-fulfilling.

FOLLOW
THE LEADER

the 30-second theory

One of history's greatest criminals, Adolf Hitler, was actually voted into power. How? A key theory has its basis in social psychologist Henri Tajfel's experiences as a prisoner of war in the Second World War. Himself a Jew, Tajfel wanted to explain how an horrific event such as the Holocaust could occur – most of his Polish relatives and friends were murdered, and Tajfel only escaped by concealing his identity. A series of experiments carried out in the 1970s helped Tajfel to recognize that people will show remarkable allegiance to arbitrary groups for seemingly unimportant reasons – shared hair colour, place of birth or even after being randomly assigned to a group by an experimenter. This is social identity theory. These groups need leaders, and US psychologist Michael Hogg in the 1990s found that group members will choose not the 'best-and-brightest', but the most *average* individuals with whom most members could easily identify. Once they're in power, by necessity leaders become different from their constituents, so they must go to increasing lengths to prove they are like their group. This may be why nationalistic slogans – and even outright racism – are often effective political strategies. By defining their group in exclusive terms, leaders can reinforce their social identity and build power.

3-SECOND PSYCHE
The best leaders are bold and charismatic, right? No, social identity theory says people tend to follow the most prototypical members of their group.

3-MINUTE ANALYSIS
What makes a person identify with one group over another? You're reading this book; does that make you a 'reader', an 'English-speaker', or a 'psychology fan'? How groups are chosen is a puzzle social psychologists continue to ponder. Social identity theory says that you may identify with any one of them, but you could be motivated by many factors, including self-esteem, reducing uncertainty or even simply because these groups are suggested to you here.

RELATED THEORIES
See also
ZIMBARDO'S PRISON
Page 76
MILGRAM'S OBEDIENCE STUDY
Page 80
STEREOTYPE THREAT
Page 82

3-SECOND BIOGRAPHIES
MICHAEL HOGG
1950–
HENRI TAJFEL
1919–1982

30-SECOND TEXT
Dave Munger

Looking and dressing like your followers can help to make you a more popular leader, fostering the sense that you are one of them.

WAYS WE DIFFER

cognitive bias The tendency for people to make false judgments based on erroneous presuppositions. There are many forms of cognitive bias, including projection bias (assuming people think the same way you do) and confirmation bias (ignoring information that does not fit in with your beliefs). Its purpose is to help the brain process information quickly, but it throws the reliability of anecdotal and personal evidence into doubt.

cognitive behavioural therapy (CBT)
A therapeutic approach that focuses on the way in which a patient thinks about and manages problems. The premise of cognitive behavioural therapy is that people have self-destructive tendencies and patterns of behaviour that are self-perpetuating and amplify, rather than solve, problems. Using workbooks to record their reaction to difficulties, patients are taught to recognize these negative patterns and are given positive strategies for dealing with problems.

dialectic construct A belief that is arrived at by considering both sides of the argument. Dialectics is the process of pitching an idea (thesis) against its opposite (antithesis) and developing a new idea that combines the two.

epigenetics The study of how cells are able to change their appearance and behaviour, despite maintaining the same DNA. It is thought that environmental factors trigger a change in gene expression (how the gene behaves), without requiring any change to its DNA imprint.

extraversion One of the big five personality traits (see page 92). Extraversion is associated with being particularly motivated by potential reward. Extraverts (also spelled extroverts) tend to be outward-going and enjoy the company of others. They look to the outside world for stimulation, rather than looking within. Everyone has aspects of all five personality traits, to varying degrees.

idiographic Concerned with specific events or facts, rather than generalities. In psychology, this means focusing on the psychological makeup of the individual person rather than seeking general theories of behaviour.

innate An essential part of something or someone, possibly existing since birth. From the Latin *innatus*, meaning to 'be born in'.

IQ test A measure of intelligence; IQ stands for intelligence quotient. The original test was devised by Alfred Binet in France in the early 1900s and adapted by American psychologist Lewis Terman in 1916. It uses a series of questions to test memory, attention and problem-solving abilities. Originally, the mental age of the subject was divided by their chronological age and multiplied by a hundred to produce the intelligence quotient. Thus, a child of 10 who has a mental age of 12 would score 12/10 x 100 = 120. The modern IQ test is standardized such that an average score is always 100.

narcissistic The tendency to be excessively preoccupied with oneself and unable to empathize or care about other people.

neuroticism One of the big five personality traits. Neuroticism is associated with a stronger reaction to aversive situations – a struggle to cope with everyday stress – and in extreme cases may lead to depression and anxiety. Everyone has aspects of all five personality traits, to varying degrees.

neurotransmitter A chemical that acts as a messenger between neurons and allows impulses to be passed from one cell to the next. Neurotransmitters can either excite or inhibit adjacent cells.

personal construct theory The idea that someone's personality is formed by their understanding of the world around them. By testing different theories to see if they work, we build up a series of 'constructs' that define our understanding of the world and create aspects of our personality. The theory was developed by American psychologist George Kelly in the 1950s. He devised a test called the 'repertory grid' whereby patients are shown three cards, chosen from a set of twenty-one, and asked to choose the odd one out. The results are entered onto a grid to reveal the patients' personal constructs.

personality test A test, usually composed of a series of questions or tasks, designed to evaluate various aspects of the subject's personality. Many different types of test are available, most of them scored using either a dimensional approach, whereby the results are measured on a scale, or a typological approach, whereby the results are matched to predetermined categories or 'types'.

THE LAKE WOBEGON EFFECT

the 30-second theory

'Mirror, mirror on the wall who is the fairest of them all?' – the immortal question asked, of course, by the narcissistic Evil Queen from the Snow White fairy tale. Countless psychological studies show that in real life most people have a touch of the Evil Queen's vanity about them. Across a huge range of measures, from good looks and popularity to driving ability and memory capacity, the typical person believes they are superior to most others. The phenomenon also appears in profession-specific contexts. Stock traders informed about the woeful performance of the average trader continue to believe in their own prognostic powers. Our collective misplaced confidence is thought to explain a number of common human foibles, including seemingly irrational health behaviours, such as smoking ('It gives other people cancer, but I'll be okay') and tardiness – just think how many projects end up late and over-budget. Illusory superiority, as it's known more formally, was nicknamed the Lake Wobegon effect after the fictional town invented by raconteur Garrison Keillor in which 'all the women are strong, all the men are good looking, and all the children are above average'.

3-SECOND PSYCHE
Across a raft of abilities and qualities the majority of us believe that we're better than most.

3-MINUTE ANALYSIS
The Lake Wobegon effect has a negative twin known as the 'worse than average' effect. This is our negatively skewed belief in our inability to succeed relative to others at particularly unusual or difficult challenges, such as juggling or unicycling. Most of us think we'll be worse than average at such tasks, presumably because we fail to acknowledge just how much other people will struggle too.

RELATED THEORIES
See also
WASON'S CONFIRMATION BIAS
Page 60
FUNDAMENTAL ATTRIBUTION ERROR
Page 94

3-SECOND BIOGRAPHY
GARRISON KEILLOR
1942–

30-SECOND TEXT
Christian Jarrett

You may not be as handsome or beautiful as you think you are, but have you ever tried juggling? You might be surprised at how good you are.

THE BIG FIVE

the 30-second theory

We can't help but form impressions about each other's personalities. We quickly deduce that others are friendly, quiet, eccentric and so on. But just how many aspects to a personality are there? The ancient Greeks believed people fall into four temperamental categories – choleric, phlegmatic, sanguine and melancholic. In the middle of the twentieth century, the British-born psychologist Raymond Cattell devised a personality test based on the idea that there are sixteen personality factors including guilt-proneness and shrewdness. Contemporary psychology has now settled on the idea that there are in fact five main factors to personality, known as the big five – extraversion, neuroticism (associated with anxiety and apprehension), conscientiousness, agreeableness and openness (associated with creativity and insight). Each factor encapsulates those aspects of personality that tend always to go together. For example, people who are sociable tend also to be talkative and assertive, as if these three traits are all manifestations of the same underlying factor, in this case extraversion. The big five factors are continuous dimensions like weight or strength. So it's not the case that we're either neurotic or we're not. Rather, we each have a certain amount of neuroticism, and the same holds true for the other factors.

3-SECOND PSYCHE
The various permutations of personality are encapsulated by five main factors, known as the big five.

3-MINUTE ANALYSIS
The big five factors are dimensions of personality that we all share. Some psychologists have taken a different ('idiographic') approach, documenting each individual's uniqueness. Best known is George Kelly and his personal construct theory. Kelly proposed that we each see the world in the context of a unique set of dialectic constructs (such as whether people are kind or not) and that by uncovering these constructs, we learn how a person sees the world.

RELATED THEORIES
See also
BIRTH ORDER
Page 36
FUNDAMENTAL ATTRIBUTION ERROR
Page 94
NATURE VIA NURTURE
Page 98
NOMINATIVE DETERMINISM
Page 104

3-SECOND BIOGRAPHIES
RAYMOND CATTELL
1905–1998
GEORGE KELLY
1905–1967

30-SECOND TEXT
Christian Jarrett

If you are a high scorer on the neurotic personality dimension, then you might be worried about the risk of those precarious blocks and numbers toppling over.

FUNDAMENTAL ATTRIBUTION ERROR

the 30-second theory

3-SECOND PSYCHE

It is easy to think of our own behaviour as caused by events, and the behaviour of others as caused by their personalities.

3-MINUTE ANALYSIS

Although fundamental attribution operates in many different situations, there are differences in how strong it is. Research into individualistic versus collectivist cultures (for example, US vs. Chinese) suggests that the bias is stronger in individualistic ones, where people have a stronger sense of themselves as independent. Anxious individuals are more prone to attribute negative events to flaws in their natures, rather than to circumstances. Cognitive behavioural therapists focus on these attributions, attempting to change the 'explanatory style' someone uses to think about the world.

Attribution is the psychological process of discerning the causes of things. The fundamental attribution error is the tendency to attribute the causes of other people's behaviour to their intrinsic natures, ignoring constraining circumstances. The phrase was coined by psychologist Lee Ross to describe results which showed that people who were asked to read out a speech on a controversial topic were then judged as holding those opinions, even by people who knew they were reading the speech because the experimenter had asked them to! The flip side of the fundamental attribution error is that we tend to overattribute our own behaviour to external circumstances, rather than to personality characteristics. In other words, 'I was late because the alarm didn't go off, but you're late because you're careless!' Or, 'your views are prejudiced, but mine are reasonable.' The fundamental attribution error is a classic cognitive bias; a tendency in people's thinking found in many situations. Critically, people also often fail to account for the effect of this bias on their thinking. The reason for this is the same as the reason why the bias exists in the first place: our own circumstances and intentions are available to us directly and feel compelling. The intentions and circumstances of others are not available to us, so we judge them on their overt behaviours.

RELATED THEORY

See also
BECK'S COGNITIVE THERAPY
Page 124

3-SECOND BIOGRAPHIES

EDWARD E. JONES
1927–1993

RICHARD NISBETT
1941–

LEE ROSS
1942–

30-SECOND TEXT

Tom Stafford

If others are late for a date do you instantly put it down to lack of good timekeeping? Fundamental attribution error suggests that people tend to blame the behaviour of others first, and not allow for mitigating circumstances.

1916
Born, Berlin

1934
Moves to Dijon, France,
then London

1938
Marries Margaret Davies

1942
Psychologist at Mill Hill
Hospital

1946
Psychologist at Maudsley
Hospital

1950
Marries Sybil Rostal

1955
Professor of Psychology,
Institute of Psychiatry

1971
Publishes *Race,
Intelligence and
Education*

1983
Retires

1990
Publishes autobiography
Rebel With a Cause

1997
Dies, London

HANS EYSENCK

Your IQ is inherited and depends on the racial group to which you belong. The position of the stars in the sky when you are born affects your personality for the rest of your life. Smoking doesn't cause lung cancer. These are a few of the more controversial beliefs championed by German-born psychologist Hans Eysenck during a lifetime of challenging the scientific establishment.

On some points, the rest of the world did eventually catch up with him. His view that Freud was unscientific and psychoanalysis does not help treat neurosis, for instance, caused outrage when he first mooted it in the 1950s, but has since gained wider support. He was also one of the first to argue that sex and violence on television have a detrimental effect on viewers, an idea derided in the 1970s but which many analysts now agree with. And what of his view that politics divide not simply into left and right, or radicalism and conservatism, but into 'tough-mindedness' and 'tender-mindedness'? According to this theory, fascists, communists, men and the working class all tend toward 'tough-mindedness', while liberals, women and the middle class are more 'tender-minded'. Not only that, but your position on the tough-tender scale is 50 per cent determined by your genes.

Perhaps not surprisingly, Eysenck's extreme views provoked extreme reactions. He was described as 'the psychologist people most love to hate' and was physically attacked while giving a speech. Eysenck, however, should also be remembered for his three-factor model of personality, which has largely stood the test of time, and acted as a forerunner to the now widely accepted big five model. His high public profile was accompanied by a prodigious output, including some eighty books, and, by the time he died, he was the most-quoted psychologist of his generation. 'Tact and diplomacy are fine in international relations, in politics, perhaps even in business,' he wrote, 'in science only one thing matters, and that is the facts.'

NATURE
VIA NURTURE

the 30-second theory

Are we born with a fixed set of traits and dispositions, or are we more like a lump of sculpting clay, moulded by the hands of life? This of course is the classic nature/nurture debate, which in modern scientific parlance has become a question of the relative contribution of genes versus the environment. Today it's recognized that humans are shaped both by their genetic inheritance and by their life's experiences, often in an interactive fashion. A great example of how genes and the environment can combine to produce a given outcome was provided by a decades-long study of thousands of people in New Zealand. During this study people were tested for the presence of a less active version of a certain gene, MAOA (which is indirectly involved with the release of neurotransmitters, such as serotonin, that control mood and aggression). In those people who had had a non-abusive upbringing, the presence of the less active MAOA gene made no difference to the likelihood of that person having an aggressive personality in adulthood. However, for participants who'd suffered maltreatment in childhood, having the less active MAOA gene made them particularly vulnerable to developing an antisocial personality. This isn't nature versus nurture, it's nature via nurture.

RELATED THEORIES
See also
EVOLUTIONARY PSYCHOLOGY
Page 24
THE BIG FIVE
Page 92
FUNDAMENTAL
ATTRIBUTION ERROR
Page 94

3-SECOND BIOGRAPHY
ROBERT PLOMIN
1948–

30-SECOND TEXT
Christian Jarrett

3-SECOND PSYCHE
It's not nature or nurture that shapes the person we become, it's both, each interacting with and influencing the other.

3-MINUTE ANALYSIS
In a further demonstration of how nature and nurture interact, cutting-edge bioscience is starting to reveal how certain experiences can alter the functioning of genes, even without changing the DNA sequence itself (an individual's unique set of genes). Known as epigenetics, it's been demonstrated, for example, that rats raised by a doting mother are less susceptible to stress because the extra preening changes the functioning of genes involved in communication between brain cells.

Mary hoped that her daughter Susan would become an airline pilot. Playing aeroplane might help, but Susan's career choices will also depend on her genes.

THE FLYNN EFFECT

the 30-second theory

3-SECOND PSYCHE
Average performance on intelligence tests increased throughout much of the twentieth century.

3-MINUTE ANALYSIS
Data from the end of the twentieth century suggest that the Flynn effect has stopped in some developed nations and may even have started to reverse. A 2008 study by Thomas Teasdale and David Owen of Danish army conscripts found that those who had their intelligence tested in 2003–4 had significantly lower IQ scores than those tested in 1998. The cause is unknown.

Humans are getting cleverer.

At least that's what appears to be happening if you compare average performance on intelligence tests today with average scores achieved by previous generations through the twentieth century. The phenomenon has been dubbed 'the Flynn effect', after the New Zealand Professor of Political Studies James R. Flynn who first noticed it. The same pattern has been found for the nearly thirty countries for which we have the necessary historical data. How big is the intelligence rise? According to Flynn, if we allocated an IQ score of 100 to the average performance of contemporary American adults (as is the convention), an American adult of average intelligence in the year 1900 would, by today's standards, achieve a score of between 50 and 70. This is the range normally considered learning disabled! Of course the Victorians weren't all stupid. Further investigation shows that it's only on certain subscales that we have improved – especially those that tap our ability to categorize concepts and recognize abstract rules. Flynn believes that it's the rising ubiquity of science education and visual technologies that have boosted our performance in these specific areas.

RELATED THEORIES
See also
NEUROPLASTICITY
Page 44
NATURE VIA NURTURE
Page 98

3-SECOND BIOGRAPHY
JAMES FLYNN
1934–

30-SECOND TEXT
Christian Jarrett

The chances are that you have a substantially higher IQ than your grandparents. But does that really mean that you're cleverer or just better at taking tests?

ERICSSON'S 10,000-HOUR RULE
the 30-second theory

It's tempting to look at truly exceptional achievers – such as Olympic athletes and celebrated musicians – and conclude that they must have been born with a unique gift for what they do. According to influential research by psychologist Anders Ericsson, however, the path to expertise is available to anyone who's prepared to put in the necessary levels of practice. How much? Studies of elite musicians, athletes and chess players suggest at least 10,000 hours of practice spread over a period of more than ten years. What's more, not just any kind of practice will do. Ericsson says it needs to be what he calls 'deliberate practice', in which you don't just repeat what you know but instead constantly seek to stretch yourself. This inevitably involves forensic self-criticism, repeated failure and a dogged ability to keep dusting yourself down and trying again – a process that's not particularly enjoyable and quite distinct from leisurely practice. Although Ericsson's perspective argues against the idea of innate gifts, his concept of deliberate practice does of course require a rare mix of motivation, good health and opportunity.

RELATED THEORIES
See also
FUNDAMENTAL ATTRIBUTION ERROR
Page 94
NATURE VIA NURTURE
Page 98

3-SECOND BIOGRAPHY
ANDERS ERICSSON
1947–

30-SECOND TEXT
Christian Jarrett

3-SECOND PSYCHE
Greatness isn't innate, it comes from epic amounts of self-critical, obsessive practice.

3-MINUTE ANALYSIS
As well as excessive practice, other situational factors that apparently ease us towards greatness include being born in January (thereby having the advantage of being older than peers in class and on the sports pitch) and being born in a city of fewer than 500,000 citizens – the latter apparently allows for the opportunity to sample many different activities, which builds generic skills, such as self-discipline and coordination.

Biographies of musical geniuses like Mozart and Michael Jackson nearly always reveal that they started relentless practice from an early age.

NOMINATIVE DETERMINISM

the 30-second theory

3-SECOND PSYCHE
Our names and initials can affect our lives in intriguing ways.

3-MINUTE ANALYSIS
Another way our names can influence our lives is via the initials that they spell out. Nicholas Christenfeld at the University of California, San Diego, analyzed thousands of California death certificates and found that men with positive initials (e.g. A.C.E.) outlived by an average of four years those with neutral initials, whereas men with negative initials (e.g. D.I.E.) died, on average, two years younger than those with neutral initials.

There's a urologist at my local hospital called Mr Waterfall. A palliative care expert at Lancaster University is called Sheila Payne, and at the University of New Mexico there's an expert on the evolutionary psychology of sexuality called Randy Thornhill. The idea that the destiny of these individuals was shaped by their names has been dubbed 'nominative determinism'. In fact there's little evidence that the meaning of our names really does influence our career choices – just think of all the people whose names don't match their professions. However, there are other ways in which our names can affect our lives. For instance, people with surnames near the start of the alphabet tend to enjoy certain benefits, such as being given more time during medical consultations. In economics, in which the authors of papers are listed in alphabetical order, there's even evidence that people with an alphabetical name advantage have more successful careers. Names that reveal a person's ethnicity can also exert an influence. Research conducted in the United States found that a résumé attributed to a black-sounding name, such as Jamal, was less likely to receive an employer response than an identical résumé attributed to a white-sounding name, such as Emily.

RELATED THEORIES
BIRTH ORDER
Page 36
THE BIG FIVE
Page 92
FUNDAMENTAL ATTRIBUTION ERROR
Page 94
NATURE VIA NURTURE
Page 98

3-SECOND BIOGRAPHY
NICHOLAS CHRISTENFELD
1963–

30-SECOND TEXT
Christian Jarrett

If your surname is Thompson, try not to give your child first and middle names beginning with R and O, respectively.

DISORDERED MINDS

Asperger's syndrome One of the milder forms of autistic spectrum disorders (ASD). Typical symptoms are physical clumsiness and social awkwardness. Emotional development is delayed, and the child might develop an obsessive interest in one subject (e.g. trains) to the exclusion of all else.

autism A condition that typically affects social behaviour, language development and learning ability, to varying degrees. The main symptoms are an inability to relate and interact with other people and an obsessive interest in one subject, to the extent that the child might become a genius in that area. Language use is restricted and the child might repeat words or phrases endlessly.

corpus callosum The mass of nerve fibres that connects the two sides of the brain and allows them to share information.

defence mechanism A usually unconscious mental process used to protect oneself from painful thoughts or feelings. On the positive side, this allows people to function socially without succumbing to their emotions. On the negative side, it can mean that painful issues aren't addressed and are expressed in other, possibly more destructive, ways. Typical defence mechanisms include denial, repression, projection and rationalization.

dissociation A usually unconscious process of compartmentalizing certain thoughts or functions to isolate them from the normal activities of the brain. The function of dissociation is to deal with traumatic thoughts or emotions and strip them of their emotional significance.

dopamine A naturally occurring chemical that is produced in several areas of the brain. As well as assisting with motor functions and concentration, it promotes feelings of euphoria and joy.

epilepsy A neurological disorder in which the electrical discharge in certain parts of the brain is disturbed, leading to recurring episodes of convulsive seizures, possibly accompanied by loss of consciousness.

hemisphere One half of the brain. The left hemisphere is associated with language processing and arithmetic skills, while the right hemisphere is associated with spatial awareness and artistic sensibility.

neurology The area of medicine that specializes in the nervous system, including the brain. Topics include the physical state of the brain, physical functions affected by the brain, such as balance, and cognitive abilities, such as memory and speech.

phobia An irrational and obsessive fear of an object, person or situation. Objects of phobias include spiders, bees, birds, water, foreigners, men, women and sex.

positive psychology A recent branch of psychology that aims to foster happiness and well-being in normal life, instead of focusing uniquely on mental illness. Pioneered by American psychologist Martin Seligman, positive psychology seeks to encourage patients' key strengths and their capacity for self-determination.

psychogenic Something, such as an illness, that has its origins in the mind rather than the body. Psychogenic illnesses may be the result of unacceptable thoughts or feelings that have been repressed by the unconscious mind and are expressed physically in the body.

psychologist Someone who practises psychology, the study of how the mind works and how mental disorders are expressed through abnormal behaviour. Unlike psychiatrists, psychologists do not usually have a medical qualification, and treatment is usually through therapy rather than medicine.

psychosis A symptom of mental illness that includes hallucinations, delusions and a distorted sense of reality. Psychosis is one of the defining characteristics of schizophrenia, as well as several other mental disorders. It can be caused by either biological or social factors, or a combination of the two.

psychotherapist A generic term for anyone who practises psychotherapy, the treatment of mental disorders through therapy – including psychiatrists, psychologists and psychiatric nurses. There are more than 250 different types of psychotherapy.

repression A defence mechanism, identified by Freud, that blocks unacceptable impulses and drives them into the unconscious mind. Freud made the point that ideas that are consciously dismissed, or 'repudiated', lose their energy, while those that are repressed retain their energy while lying dormant in the unconscious.

schizophrenia A psychological disorder thought to be caused by a chemical imbalance in the brain. Typically, the condition is marked by a distorted view of reality, an inability to function socially, withdrawal from society, hearing voices and delusions of grandeur.

SPERRY'S SPLIT BRAINS

the 30-second theory

The brain has two hemispheres, left and right, each of which is connected and coordinated across a bundle of fibres called the corpus callosum. During the 1960s, the neuroscientist Roger Sperry discovered that when this bundle is severed, the human brain not only continues to function, but each side is, to some degree, independently conscious. Sperry was studying patients with seemingly untreatable epilepsy who had had their corpus callosum surgically cut in an attempt to stop seizures spreading. Many years before, neuroscientists examining patients with brain damage had discovered that certain functions, such as language, were more reliant on the left hemisphere, whereas visual abilities were more reliant on the right. Sperry realized that 'split brain' patients allowed these differences to be explored in detail. He found, for example, that a word presented to the language-specialized left hemisphere was read and understood as normal, whereas a word presented to the language-minimal right hemisphere went unrecognized. But when the task was to draw what the word described, the patient could produce sketches from words presented to the visual-arrangement-specialized right hemisphere, but not the other way around.

RELATED THEORY
See also
CONSCIOUSNESS
Page 150

3-SECOND BIOGRAPHY
ROGER SPERRY
1913–1994

30-SECOND TEXT
Vaughan Bell

3-SECOND PSYCHE
When the brain's hemispheres are surgically divided, consciousness can be split in subtle and interesting ways.

3-MINUTE ANALYSIS
Popular culture got carried away with Sperry's discoveries and we often hear the inaccurate idea that the right side of the brain is 'creative' while the left side is 'logical'. These are general tendencies, not absolutes, and are about as useful as suggesting that people from one country are 'emotional' while those from another country are 'practical'. If anything, Sperry's work highlighted that the brain is a complex network and that our abilities rely on the coordination of both hemispheres for their full potential.

The next time you're in two minds about something, spare a thought for those epilepsy patients with a severed corpus callosum, literally splitting their minds in two.

SELIGMAN'S PREPARED LEARNING

the 30-second theory

Snake and spider phobias are much more common than morbid fears about traffic or electric sockets, despite the fact that cars and electricity kill many more people. Psychologist Martin Seligman's prepared learning theory suggests that this is because we have developed a fear system that is 'prepared' – sensitive to certain situations due to the effect of evolution. In the modern world, traffic and electrical accidents are major killers, but for the majority of the history of primates (our early ancestors), hazards such as snakes and spiders have been a far greater risk. According to the theory, individual primates who more easily learned to fear the biggest threats were those more likely to survive and pass on their genes – meaning, over time, that we have evolved a genetically based, fear-learning system that is tuned to certain dangers and not others. Seligman came up with his theory in 1970, but years of subsequent experiments have backed up the idea with evidence suggesting that this sensitivity can be detected even in monkeys and babies, so demonstrating its innateness. The theory has also evolved, with more recent versions suggesting that evolution has given us a specific 'fear module' that works quickly, automatically and relies on dedicated brain circuits.

RELATED THEORIES
See also
WATSON'S BEHAVIOURISM
Page 16
EVOLUTIONARY PSYCHOLOGY
Page 24
PAVLOV'S DOGS
Page 134

3-SECOND BIOGRAPHY
MARTIN E.P. SELIGMAN
1942 –

30-SECOND TEXT
Vaughan Bell

3-SECOND PSYCHE
We've been shaped by evolution to fear those objects and situations – such as snakes and heights – that were a threat to our distant ancestors.

3-MINUTE ANALYSIS
While the notion that some fears are more easily learned than others is generally accepted, the claim that this is purely a result of evolutionary processes has been more difficult to prove. As phobias do not typically appear until adolescence or adulthood, it's possible we are more likely to fear certain things as much because of cultural beliefs, through observing how other people react and warnings given by parents, as through the effect of evolution.

A healthy dose of arachnophobia may have saved your ancestors' skin, allowing the trait to be passed onto you.

CHARCOT'S HYSTERIA

the 30-second theory

The French neurologist

Jean-Martin Charcot discovered that some patients who appeared to have neurological problems – paralysis, blindness, epileptic seizures – in fact had no damage to the brain or nerves that could explain their difficulties. Although the patients had no conscious control over their symptoms, some could be temporarily 'cured' through hypnosis, leading Charcot to believe that the unconscious was blocking access to other functions of the brain. The idea was revolutionary because it brought the idea of the unconscious into the mainstream of medical thought and overturned almost 2000 years of belief that hysteria was a female condition, originally thought by the Ancient Greeks to be caused by a 'wandering womb'. Two of Charcot's students extended the concept: Pierre Janet suggested that the mind could 'dissociate' or compartmentalize different functions, while Sigmund Freud suggested that this occurred when traumatic memories were converted into physical symptoms as a way of repressing them from the conscious mind. Although there is still little evidence that Freudian repression is responsible, the idea that medical symptoms as serious as blindness and paralysis can be caused by the unconscious mind is now widely accepted.

3-SECOND PSYCHE
Striking physical symptoms, such as blindness and paralysis, can be caused by the unconscious mind blocking access to essential brain functions.

3-MINUTE ANALYSIS
Modern neuroscience suggests that 'hysterical' or 'psychogenic' symptoms, as they are called now, might be caused by the frontal lobes impeding other brain functions. It is still not clear exactly why this happens, but we know that patients with these symptoms often have other emotional difficulties. This suggests that psychogenic symptoms are not working as an effective 'defence mechanism', as Freud proposed, but they may be triggered by emotion in other ways.

RELATED THEORY
See also
PSYCHOANALYSIS
Page 18

3-SECOND BIOGRAPHIES
JEAN-MARTIN CHARCOT
1825–1893

SIGMUND FREUD
1856–1939

PIERRE JANET
1859–1947

30-SECOND TEXT
Vaughan Bell

To say that a person's illness is 'all in their mind' doesn't mean that they are making it up. They could be suffering from a form of hysteria.

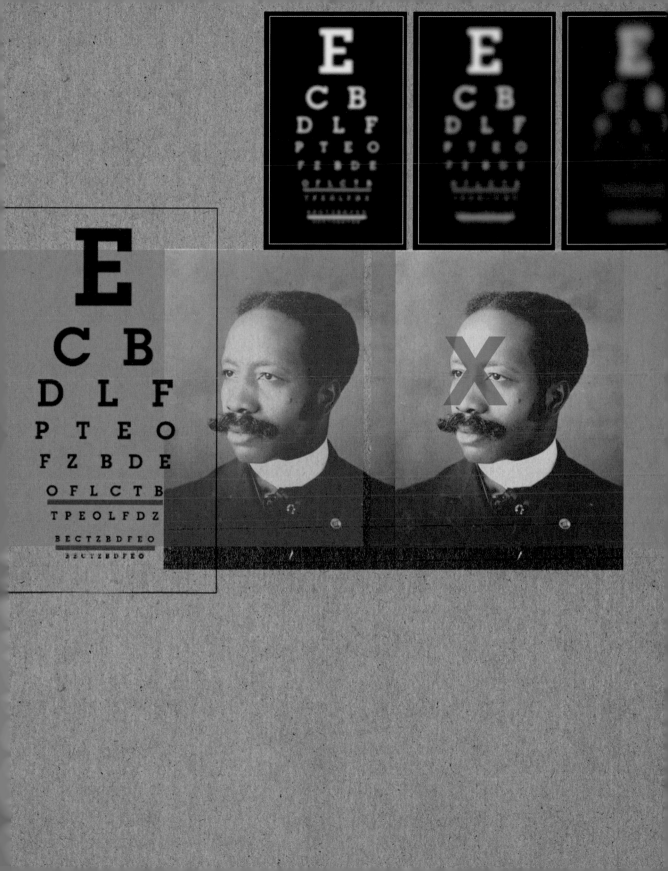

ROSENHAN'S INSANE PLACES

the 30-second theory

3-SECOND PSYCHE
'If sanity and insanity exist, how shall we know them?' asked David Rosenhan's 1973 study, in which fake patients with unlikely symptoms were diagnosed with schizophrenia.

3-MINUTE ANALYSIS
Psychiatrist Robert Spitzer replied that if he drank blood and vomited in an emergency room to fake a peptic ulcer, the staff should not be blamed for being misled and nor should they change the definition of internal bleeding. Despite making this criticism, Spitzer led a reform of how mental illnesses are defined and modern diagnoses are now much less vague or subject to individual interpretation.

In the early 1970s David Rosenhan believed that the medical definitions of mental illness were hopelessly vague and subject to the whims of the individual doctor. He decided to test how well psychiatrists could distinguish between 'sane' and 'insane' people by sending eight friends to hospital emergency rooms, each pretending to hear a voice saying 'empty', 'hollow', and 'thud'. All eight were diagnosed with schizophrenia and admitted to psychiatric hospitals, at which point, following Rosenhan's earlier instructions, they began to act normally and report that their 'voices' had gone. The 'pseudopatients' were kept in hospital, often for weeks, while staff consistently interpreted normal behaviour as part of their non-existent illness. When news of the study spread, a local university hospital doubted that it would make such errors so Rosenhan promised to send more fake patients. In reality, he sent none, but in the meantime the hospital had branded more than forty real patients as fakers and another twenty-three were regarded as suspect. The shockwaves from the study, provocatively entitled 'On Being Sane in Insane Places', battered the confidence of the medical profession and led to a new system of diagnosis that depends on checklists and scientific studies that test how reliably psychiatrists can use them.

RELATED THEORIES
See also
WASON'S CONFIRMATION BIAS
Page 60
JANIS' GROUPTHINK
Page 72

3-SECOND BIOGRAPHIES
DAVID ROSENHAN
1931–
ROBERT SPITZER
1932–

30-SECOND TEXT
Vaughan Bell

Is it fair to tell doctors about fake symptoms and then complain when the result is an inappropriate diagnosis? Rosenhan's shock study led to a more rigorous system of diagnosis for mental illness.

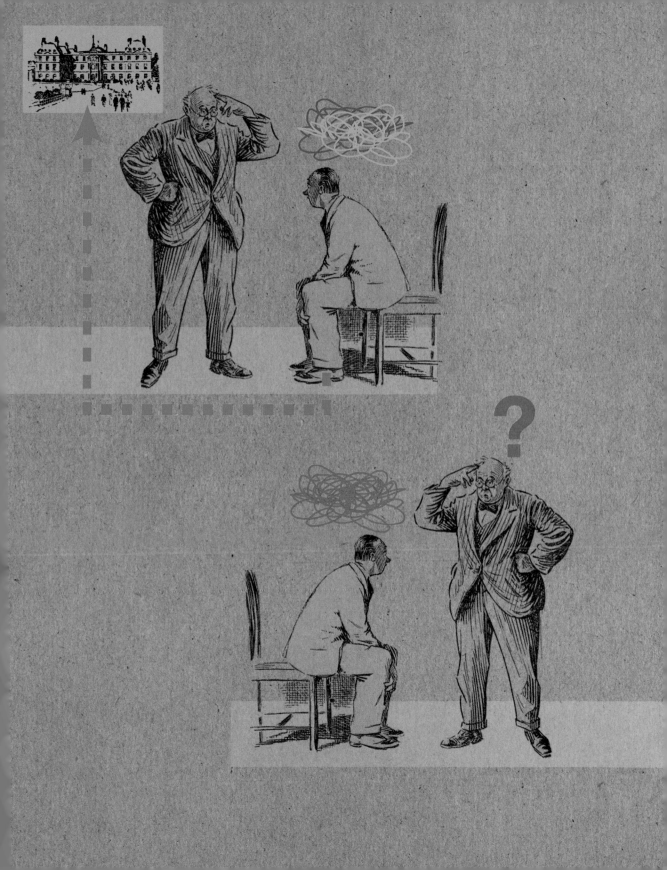

1921
Born, Providence, Rhode Island

1946
Ph.D. in Psychiatry from Yale Medical School

1950
Marries Phyllis Whitman

1950
Works at Austen Riggs Center, Massachusetts

1954
Joins University of Philadelphia

1971
Professor of Psychology at University of Philadelphia

1975
Publishes *Cognitive Therapy and the Emotional Disorders*

1994
Establishes the Beck Institute of Cognitive Therapy

2006
Wins Lasker Clinical Research Award

2007
Short-listed for Nobel Prize in Medicine

AARON BECK

Who killed Sigmund Freud?

The short answer, metaphorically speaking, must be Aaron Beck. When Beck qualified in psychiatry in 1946, psychoanalysis was in its heyday, and the profession was dominated by persuasive characters who ruled the roost through 'eminence' rather than 'evidence'. The only reliable measure was a rule of thumb, which said that about a third of patients would get better, a third would get worse and a third would stay the same.

Beck changed all that. He devised a series of clinical trials that put psychoanalytical theories to the test. In each case, the theories failed to match the experience of real-life patients. Subsequent trials lead him to develop his own approach which, allied to the ideas of the behaviourists, would become known as cognitive behavioural therapy (or CBT). Crucially, however, Beck didn't merely prove Freud wrong and offer an alternative, he created tests to measure the effectiveness of treatments, and backed his ideas up with empirical data. As a result, many of the tests used in psychotherapy today have his name attached to them, such as the Beck Depression Inventory, the Beck Hopelessness Scale, the Beck Scale for Suicidal Ideation and the Beck Anxiety Inventory. Almost single-handedly, Beck transformed psychotherapy from an art into a science.

Not surprisingly, the psychoanalytic community shunned him. Even after he qualified as a psychoanalyst, the American Psychoanalytic Institute turned down his application for membership because, in their view, his desire to carry out tests proved he had been incorrectly analyzed. But Beck's approach chimed with the larger society, with its desire for scientific evidence and pragmatic solutions rather than the long, quasi-mysterious explorations of psychoanalysis. Within a few decades, Freud's ideas would be almost completely superseded by Beck's: The king was dead; long live the king.

KAPUR'S ABERRANT SALIENCE

the 30-second theory

3-SECOND PSYCHE
In psychosis, the brain chemical dopamine is overactive causing affected people to perceive irrelevant things as important and attention-grabbing.

3-MINUTE ANALYSIS
The risk of mental illness is not fully explained by what we know about brain chemicals and evidence suggests that a whole host of traits and experiences play a part – including a family history of mental illness, living environment, personal relationships, lifetime stress and even birth complications. Neuroscience is an important tool but we need to appreciate the whole person to best understand and support people who are mentally distressed.

Psychosis is a mind-bending state in which people develop delusions and hallucinations as part of mental illnesses such as schizophrenia. Medically speaking, delusions are unfounded yet unshakeable beliefs that are not just a case of being mistaken – they can include states such as believing that your thoughts are being stolen with microwaves, or that secret agents are controlling your actions. Aberrant salience theory, developed by psychiatrist Shitij Kapur, aims to explain how reality starts breaking down in psychosis on the basis that affected people often show changes in the brain's use of a chemical messenger called dopamine. Kapur argues that the neurochemical is involved in highlighting which things are 'motivationally important'. In other words, it works like the contrast control on a television, but instead of changing how sharply light and dark stand out from each other, it changes how 'salient' or important things seem. For example, normally, if you're hungry, food grabs your attention to a heightened degree. Aberrant salience theory says that problems with dopamine cause this system to go wrong, with the result that those affected start noticing irrelevant things and believe them to be incredibly important, leading to strange and compelling delusions that alter their behaviour.

RELATED THEORIES
See also
WASON'S CONFIRMATION BIAS
Page 60
LOFTUS' FALSE MEMORIES
Page 140

3-SECOND BIOGRAPHY
SHITIJ KAPUR
1964–

30-SECOND TEXT
Vaughan Bell

A CCTV camera seems to be pointing right at you – coincidence or conspiracy? Faulty brain chemistry can lead people to think the latter.

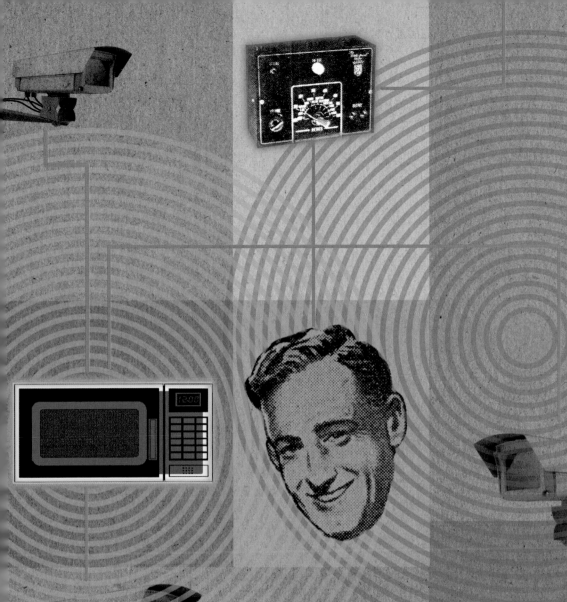

MASLOW'S HUMANISTIC PSYCHOLOGY

the 30-second theory

3-SECOND PSYCHE

Humans strive for personal growth and self-realization despite the challenges of life, and psychology needs to incorporate these aspects to fully understand human nature.

3-MINUTE ANALYSIS

Although Maslow was critical of the narrow focus of scientific psychology, he always saw the humanistic approach as a complement to it, rather than as a replacement, and remained a little disappointed that his ideas were not more influential among scientists of the time. Recently, however, the theme of human potential and happiness has been picked up by the more scientifically minded positive psychology movement which cites Maslow as an early inspiration.

Abraham Maslow trained as an experimental psychologist but became disillusioned with defining human nature through lab experiments and was dissatisfied with the Freudian alternative. Instead of seeing humans as the passive recipients of experience or slaves to unconscious drives, Maslow saw us as motivated by an ultimate need to become fulfilled and 'self-actualized', where we are at peace with ourselves and others and have the psychological freedom 'to become everything that one is capable of becoming'. Humanistic psychology grew from this inspiration and placed subjective lived experience, rather than the unconscious mind, at the centre of human nature. Many psychotherapists pursued these ideas, most notably Carl Rogers, who based 'client-centred therapy' on the principles of genuineness and acceptance of a person's basic worth. Although Maslow was sometimes uncomfortable with how his approach was adopted by the 1960s counter-culture, leading to everything from love-ins to nude psychotherapy, his central themes of respect for individual autonomy and the encouragement of personal development are now at the core of most modern psychological treatments and his 'hierarchy of needs' is still considered an important theory of human motivation.

RELATED THEORIES

WATSON'S BEHAVOURISM
Page 16
PSYCHOANALYSIS
Page 18
POSITIVE PSYCHOLOGY
Page 26

3-SECOND BIOGRAPHY

ABRAHAM H. MASLOW
1908–1970

30-SECOND TEXT

Vaughan Bell

Wallowing at the bottom of Maslow's hierarchy of needs are bodily cravings like hunger and lust, and functions like sleep and excretion. At the summit is 'self-actualization' or fulfilling your potential.

BECK'S COGNITIVE THERAPY

the 30-second theory

3-SECOND PSYCHE
Mental illness involves self-defeating habits of thinking that distort how we make sense of the world. Cognitive therapy allows us to detect these patterns and use alternatives.

3-MINUTE ANALYSIS
In his early work, Beck had an unfortunate tendency to refer to more 'rational' ways of thinking, rather than more helpful ways, and this has come under criticism, as 'rationality' is a logical ideal that we don't need in order to be mentally healthy. Furthermore, the style of cognitive therapy doesn't suit everyone and so it is important to find a type of therapy that suits a person's personal preferences.

As a young psychiatrist, Aaron Beck trained as a Freudian psychoanalyst but began asking the one question that has come to define cognitive therapy: 'What's the evidence for that?' Before Beck, psychotherapy was more philosophy than science, with innovations being based on personal insight and the influence of 'big thinkers'. Beck's innovation was to develop cognitive therapy on the basis of scientific studies that tested out common assumptions. This 'testing out' approach is also recommended to patients as the treatment is based on the idea – and, in fact, the evidence – that mental illness involves biases in how we perceive, act and think about the world – some of which can be seen in the thoughts that pass through our minds and some of which we might not be aware of. For example, someone suffering from depression might tend to interpret everyday disappointments as a sign that they are 'worthless' while someone with a fear of embarrassing themselves in public might avoid social gatherings and so never learn that their worry is unrealistic. A cognitive therapist will work with the client to identify where their thinking and behaviour prevents them from getting better and will help develop strategies to overcome these problems, each of which is tested to see if it helps.

RELATED THEORY
See also
PSYCHOANALYSIS
Page 18

3-SECOND BIOGRAPHY
AARON T. BECK
1921–

30-SECOND TEXT
Vaughan Bell

Cognitive behavorial therapy helps the patient to understand and break thought patterns that trigger many psychological disorders.

EXTREME MALE BRAINS

the 30-second theory

3-SECOND PSYCHE
Autism is an exaggeration of certain male-typical traits, most notably 'systematizing' – a tendency to try to understand things by their component parts.

3-MINUTE ANALYSIS
Alternative theories suggest that the autistic brain might have a general difficulty with making sense of the 'big picture' or that the process of coordinating different mental functions may not be operating smoothly. Indeed, the diagnoses of 'autism' and 'Asperger's syndrome' involve social impairment, communication difficulties, and repetitive behaviours and there is now good evidence that these difficulties are not caused by the same things – so the whole picture is likely to be more complex than just systematizing.

Psychologist Simon Baron-Cohen argues that men tend to be 'systematizers', who attempt to understand the world through the rules by which individual parts interact, while women are better 'empathizers', who are more able to understand the emotions of others. The division, however, is not absolute, but a general trend. Baron-Cohen has collected evidence that, for example, girls can pick up on others' emotions earlier than boys, while boys can make sense of objects and spatial information at an earlier age. People with autism or a variant, such as Asperger's syndrome, can be severely impaired at understanding how others think, feel and behave but can be much better at understanding systems. Even in those with learning disabilities, this tendency can express itself as a 'special interest' in something such as a transport system, sports statistics or electrical wiring, while, in other cases, it can appear as an exceptional ability in maths, science or computers. Baron-Cohen suspects that people with autism may have been exposed to an excess of testosterone before birth that caused the systematizing tendency to operate at full volume with empathizing barely present. According to Baron-Cohen, this might also explain why autism and its variants are much more common in males.

RELATED THEORY
See also
NEUROPLASTICITY
Page 44

3-SECOND BIOGRAPHY
SIMON BARON-COHEN
1958–

30-SECOND TEXT
Vaughan Bell

If you seriously enjoy taking watches and radios to bits to find out how they work, then you're a high scorer in what Baron-Cohen calls 'systematizing' – a stereotypically male trait that is often exhibited by people with autism.

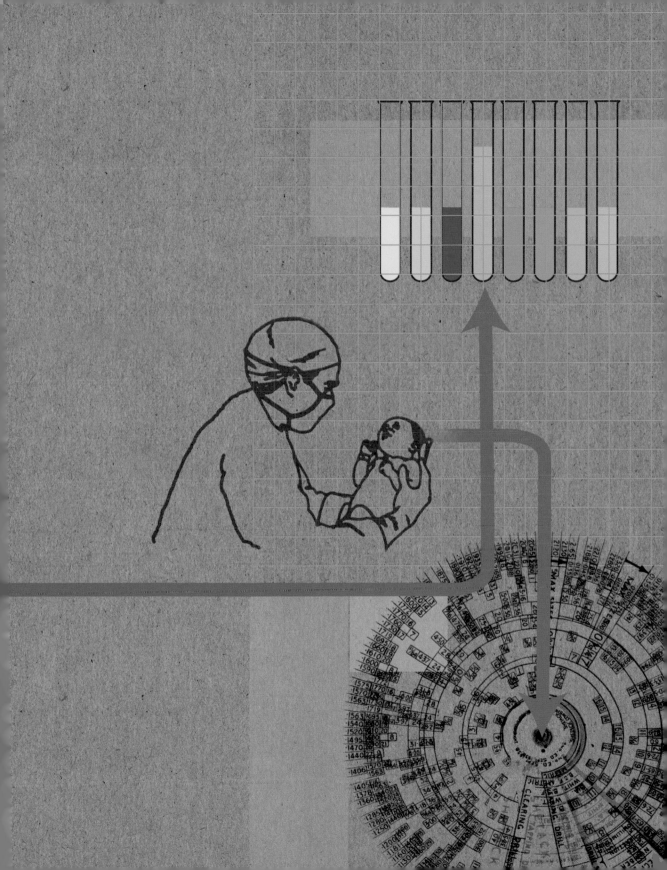

THOUGHTS & LANGUAGE

classical conditioning A learning process whereby a response is triggered through association. The most famous example is Pavlov's dogs. By ringing a bell every time the dog is presented with food, the dog comes to associate the sound of the bell with food and starts to salivate whenever it is rung.

coma A deep, often prolonged state of unconsciousness during which the patient is unable to respond to any external stimuli.

generative linguistics A school of thought in linguistics which suggests that language has innate structures and rules that are universally understood by all speakers. The idea was developed by Noam Chomsky in the 1960s and sparked a growth in the study of linguistics.

global workspace theory An explanation of the way the brain accesses multiple mental functions at the same time. It is usually described as a theatre, with the stage being the conscious mind. A spotlight illuminates the current focus of one's thoughts, while the rest of the stage is half-lit, representing thoughts on the periphery of the conscious mind. The audience is the passive, unconscious mind observing the performance, while other mental functions perform their duties backstage.

long-term memory The brain's capacity to store information for long periods – possibly an entire lifetime. Short-term memory can become long-term through a process of repetition and meaningful association. Long-term memory divides into two broad categories: episodic (literal memory of events) and semantic (generic skills and information that can be used at different occasions).

operant conditioning A learning process whereby behaviour is influenced through a system of reward and punishment. This can take the form of positive or negative reinforcement, in which a reward is given or a penalty removed to encourage certain behaviour. Or it can take the form of positive or negative punishment, whereby a punishment is threatened or a reward is removed to discourage certain behaviour. The theory was developed by US psychologist B.F. Skinner in the 1950s.

opioid receptor A group of molecules that painkillers can lock onto and which reduces the ability of a cell to send 'pain' messages to the brain. Opioid receptors are found in the spinal column and the medial thalamus area of the brain, both of which are associated with pain detection. 'Opioid' refers to any opium-like chemical, so opioid receptor simply means the receiver of opium-like substances.

persistent vegetative state The condition of someone who has come out of a coma but shows no signs of awareness, and has not done so for at least four weeks. 'Vegetative state' refers to someone who has been in this condition for less than four weeks. Unlike someone in a coma, a patient in a persistent vegetative state can open their eyes and displays sleep-wake cycles. If the condition persists for at least a year, it becomes a permanent vegetative state.

phonology The study of the sound system of a language and how these sounds function and convey meaning. This differs from phonetics, which is concerned with the physical way these sounds are produced and received.

semantics The study of the meaning of language. Semantics differs from syntax in that it focuses on the meaning given to words and how that relates to the objects they describe, whereas syntax is concerned with the actual structure of language.

short-term memory The brain's capacity to store information for short periods – according to most studies for as little as 20–30 seconds. Short-term memory (also known as working memory) is important for remembering specific information, such as a phone number, before writing it down or consigning it to long-term memory through repetition. It also helps with functional activities, such as remembering what was at the beginning of a sentence when you reach its end.

syntax The rules that govern the structure of language. Syntax is not concerned with what the words mean, only how they are arranged and formed.

THE PLACEBO EFFECT

the 30-second theory

3-SECOND PSYCHE
The mere expectation that a treatment will make you better is enough to set in train beneficial physiological processes in the brain and body.

3-MINUTE ANALYSIS
The placebo effect has an evil twin known as the nocebo effect. This is when the expectation of harm or pain becomes a self-fulfilling prophesy, even in the absence of any known physical effect. One candidate for the nocebo effect is the discomfort some people report experiencing after using mobile phones. Scientists have failed to identify a physical cause, so it's possible the adverse effects are caused by negative beliefs about the technology.

Expectations and context play an important role in how we respond to illness and in the effect that treatments have on us. The US anaesthesiologist Henry Beecher noticed this during the Second World War. Injured troops awaiting their return home displayed far less pain than usual. The reason, Beecher surmised, was that their injuries had come to signify a positive outcome. Similarly, the placebo effect is the benefit that arises from merely expecting a treatment will be beneficial. In drug trials, pharmaceutical companies have to test their products against inert sugar pills to show that any benefit is more than just the placebo effect. Some drugs, such as diazepam (for treating anxiety), are more powerful than placebo but only if the patient is told what the drug is for – in other words, the drug acts as a placebo amplifier. Similarly, morphine is less effective if the patient is unaware they are receiving it. The placebo effect is not 'all in the mind'. In the context of pain it works via the release of the brain's own inbuilt painkillers – the opioids. If the brain's opioid receptors are blocked with a drug called naloxone, the placebo effect disappears.

RELATED THEORIES
See also
POSITIVE PSYCHOLOGY
Page 26
STEREOTYPE THREAT
Page 82

3-SECOND BIOGRAPHY
HENRY BEECHER
1904–1976

30-SECOND TEXT
Christian Jarrett

Even the colour of a pill can influence its effectiveness. Stimulants are more effective if they're red, sedatives work better when they're blue.

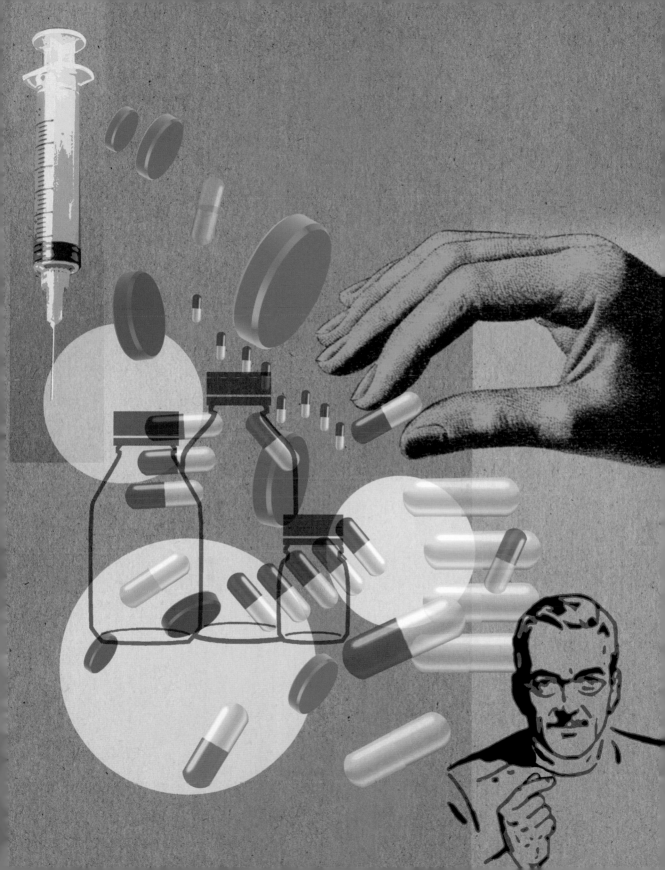

PAVLOV'S DOGS

the 30-second theory

Ivan Pavlov was the Russian

scientist who first described this fundamental law of learning. His famous demonstration involved consistently ringing a bell before feeding dogs in his laboratory. After this training, the dogs would salivate merely at the sound of the bell. This experiment demonstrated that the dogs had learned an association between two stimuli – the bell and the food. Learning this kind of association is called 'classical', or Pavlovian, conditioning. Classical conditioning doesn't just occur in dogs. It has been shown in everything from sea slugs to humans. It is important because it is one of the simplest forms of learning, but one that allows us to predict or anticipate what we're going to experience. It has also been a valuable starting point for neuroscientists interested in the biological basis for memories. Theories of classical conditioning describe how the association between two stimuli strengthens or weakens depending on how often they are presented together, how quickly one is presented before the other and whether any other stimuli are presented.

3-SECOND PSYCHE
If two things repeatedly co-occur, our brains learn to predict one to follow from the other.

3-MINUTE ANALYSIS
Note that classical conditioning doesn't account for what an animal does – it describes a situation where the stimuli are experienced regardless of how the animal acts. 'Operant conditioning' is the counterpoint to classical conditioning and describes situations in which the occurrence of stimuli (e.g. the food) is contingent on the behaviour of the animal (e.g. whether it begs or not). Operant conditioning arguably describes a broader range of learning phenomena than classical conditioning.

RELATED THEORIES
See also
WATSON'S BEHAVIOURISM
Page 16
NEUROPLASTICITY
Page 44

3-SECOND BIOGRAPHY
IVAN PAVLOV
1849–1936

30-SECOND TEXT
Tom Stafford

Dog training depends on the principles of classical and operant conditioning. The animal will obey various commands if it expects a reward to follow.

THE SAPIR–WHORF HYPOTHESIS

the 30-second theory

You've probably heard the myth about Eskimos being able to tell the difference between countless types of snow. According to the Sapir–Whorf hypothesis (named after the US linguist Edward Sapir and his student Benjamin Whorf), the reason for this proverbial ability is that Eskimos have many more words for snow than do speakers of other languages. By this account, the words we have at our disposal literally determine what we are capable of thinking and perceiving. The idea proved hugely influential for many decades after Whorf first proposed it in MIT's *Technology Review* magazine in 1940. By the 1990s, however, the hypothesis was no longer taken seriously in mainstream circles. The psychologist Steven Pinker even wrote an 'obituary' for it in his 1994 book *The Language Instinct*. Of course if we were only able to think of things for which we had the words, how would we ever learn language in the first place? The Eskimo myth has it the wrong way around – the proverbial Eskimo can't tell snow types apart because of all the snow words she knows; she uses more snow words because she's learned to recognize different snow types.

Did you develop a self-concept and then learn the word 'I' or vice versa? The Sapir–Whorf hypothesis argues that the word came first.

CHOMSKY'S UNIVERSAL GRAMMAR

the 30-second theory

RELATED THEORIES
See also
THE COGNITIVE REVOLUTION
Page 22
EVOLUTIONARY PSYCHOLOGY
Page 24
SAPIR–WHORF HYPOTHESIS
Page 136

3-SECOND PSYCHE
All languages share the same broad grammatical principles – a 'universal grammar' that is innately understood by all healthy humans and which enables us to acquire language.

3-MINUTE ANALYSIS
In school, most of us are taught 'grammar' that emphasizes the specific rules of our language: add 's' to form a plural, use an apostrophe to indicate a possessive. Chomsky and his followers aren't interested in these rules, which vary from language to language. Instead, they focus on rules that are common to all languages: sentences include noun phrases and verb phrases, which can be divided into smaller units or combined into bigger ones, then used to generate actual spoken words.

Nearly every sentence – even simple ones – can have many different meanings. For example, 'I know students like pizza' could mean (among other things) I'm aware that students enjoy pizza, or that I'm as familiar with students as I am with pizza. When US linguist Noam Chomsky was in graduate school in the 1950s, linguists had no way to explain how each sentence can have many possible meanings. Chomsky argued that this was because spoken or written language was the outward expression of a much deeper mental structure – a 'universal grammar' – shared by all humans, regardless of their language. Chomsky and his followers believe that grammar has three components: syntactical, phonological and semantic. Of these, only syntax (structure) is fundamental. Phonology (the sound of spoken words) and semantics (the meaning of sentences) are secondary. Syntax reflects the underlying structure of the mind, while phonology and semantics are arbitrary. Paradoxically, syntax is an unconscious mental process; thus, the parts of language that seem most concrete – the words and their meanings – are least interesting to Chomsky. This theory revolutionized linguistics: Chomsky's 'generative linguistics' was flexible enough to explain both the many different meanings of a sentence, and the many different languages in the world.

3-SECOND BIOGRAPHY
NOAM CHOMSKY
1928–

30-SECOND TEXT
Dave Munger

Chomsky believes that all languages share a 'universal grammar'. Some linguists have challenged the claim that all languages share the same word classes.

LOFTUS' FALSE MEMORIES

the 30-second theory

3-SECOND PSYCHE

Memories are highly malleable and easily distorted by suggestion and misinformation.

3-MINUTE ANALYSIS

Critics argued that the shopping centre incident may actually have occurred. Perhaps the parents had forgotten or never knew, and the interviews awakened in the participants a real memory of a real incident. Loftus devised the perfect rebuttal. She and her colleagues recreated their shopping centre study but this time numerous participants recalled the time they met Bugs Bunny at Disneyland – an event that couldn't possibly have happened because Bugs is a Warner Brothers' character.

On the campaign trail to become the Democratic presidential candidate in 2008, Hillary Clinton recalled her 1996 visit to Bosnia: 'I remember landing under sniper fire. There was supposed to be some kind of greeting ceremony... but instead we just ran with our heads down.' In fact, photographs of the visit show there was no sniper fire and the usual runway ceremony had taken place. Clinton admitted she'd made a mistake, she'd had a different memory. Experiencing a false memory in this way can happen to any of us because, far from being written in stone, our memories are like reconstructions, easily distorted and highly malleable. The pioneer in this field is the psychologist Elizabeth Loftus. Her seminal work involved interviewing participants about incidents from their childhood – incidents that they knew had been disclosed earlier to the research team by their parents. Among several true childhood experiences, Loftus inserted the entirely fabricated incident in which the participant had got lost in a shopping centre. Over several interviews, around a quarter of the participants came to believe that this imaginary event had really occurred, to the extent that they embellished the account with details from their own 'memory'.

RELATED THEORIES

See also
NEUROPLASTICITY
Page 44
CHARCOT'S HYSTERIA
Page 114
THE PLACEBO EFFECT
Page 132

3-SECOND BIOGRAPHY
ELIZABETH LOFTUS
1944–

30-SECOND TEXT
Christian Jarrett

Our memories are so fragile and suggestible that even the way we're asked a question can alter our precise recollection.

1944
Born Elizabeth Fishman, Los Angeles, California

1967
M.A. in psychology from Stanford University

1968
Marries Geoffrey Russell Loftus

1970
Ph.D. in psychology from Stanford University

1973
Assistant Professor, University of Washington

1979
Professor of Psychology, University of Washington

1994
Publishes *The Myth of Repressed Memory*

1998
President of the Association for Psychological Science

2002
Distinguished Professor, University of California, Irvine

ELIZABETH LOFTUS

Anyone who speaks on behalf of alleged rapists, child-killers and mass murderers is likely to make enemies. Yet this is what Elizabeth Loftus has done for much of her working life. As a result, she has been the target of public vilification, hate mail and even death threats. The reason for all this venom? Loftus is one of the prime proponents of false memory syndrome. As such, she has consulted on or appeared as an expert witness in trials as varied as those of Ted Bundy, O.J. Simpson, the Menendez brothers, Bosnian war criminals and Michael Jackson. In the process, she has spoken on behalf of people accused of unspeakable crimes – and saved many innocent people from wrongful conviction.

It all started simply enough. Pursuing her interest in memory and its links with semantics, Loftus applied for a grant from the US Department of Transport to study how people remembered car accidents.

She found that changing a single word in a question (for example, 'hit' and 'smashed', or 'a' and 'the') could yield dramatically different accounts of an event – enough to convict or acquit an accused person. When applied to murder or rape trials, the results were even more significant. Her studies were published widely in a vast number of academic journals, and she was soon in demand as an expert on unreliable memory.

As if her own studies didn't provide evidence enough, she received proof of her theories much closer to home. Thirty years after her mother drowned in a swimming pool, her uncle told her that she had been the first person to find her body. Revisiting the event in her mind, Loftus remembered everything in great detail, only to be told three days later her uncle had made a mistake and it was her aunt who had actually found her mother. Loftus had herself been susceptible to false memories.

EMBODIED COGNITION

the 30-second theory

Are you managing to grasp the ideas in this book? I don't mean are you literally holding them in your hand. I was speaking metaphorically about your comprehension. This use of physical metaphor to discuss abstract concepts is something we do a lot – we speak of employees climbing up the career ladder, of meetings being pushed forward, of weighty arguments and heated debates. The theory of embodied cognition claims that we do this because our thoughts are rooted in the physical, and in particular in our bodies. Supporting this idea is research showing how the physical world can influence our thoughts. Washing our hands makes us harsher moral judges. Placing marbles onto a higher shelf, rather than a lower one, makes it easier for people to recall positive stories. And the causal direction can run the other way too, such that our thoughts can affect our perception. Students told that a book was vital to their curriculum subsequently estimated that it was heavier than students told that the book was irrelevant. The strongest advocate for the importance of metaphor is the linguist George Lakoff. He believes we are only able to understand abstract concepts through our use of metaphor.

3-SECOND PSYCHE
We think about abstract concepts, such as time and space, in terms of physical metaphors; in turn, physical sensations can affect our thoughts and beliefs.

3-MINUTE ANALYSIS
Findings in embodied cognition have intriguing implications for the art of persuasion. Study participants tested in a warm room reported feeling socially closer to the experimenter. Participants asked to hold a glass of iced coffee rated a researcher to be more aloof. Holding a heavy clipboard led participants to rate a foreign currency more highly. Plenty for marketers to get their teeth into, so to speak!

RELATED THEORIES
See also
THE COGNITIVE REVOLUTION
Page 22
NEUROPLASTICITY
Page 44
NOMINATIVE DETERMINISM
Page 104
SAPIR–WHORF HYPOTHESIS
Page 136

3-SECOND BIOGRAPHY
GEORGE LAKOFF
1941–

30-SECOND TEXT
Christian Jarrett

There's some tentative evidence that heavier people possess a greater sense of self-importance – another example of embodiment interacting with the mind's metaphors.

Abutebaris modo subjunctivo
libertatem est vendere
absentem laedit
crede quod hal
parturient montes, nascetur ridiculus mus
aut viam
magnus acervus erit
accipere quam
adde parvum parvo
dulce bellum inexpertis
facere praestat
crede quod habes, et habes
Acta est fabula, plaudite!
beneficium accipere
parturient montes,
dulce bellum inexpertis
inveniam aut faciam
100.00
TIMER ADVANCE
TIMER SET
100.00

BROADBENT'S BOTTLENECK

the 30-second theory

In a crowded cocktail party, dozens of people might be speaking at the same time. Yet most of us are able to follow a single conversation while ignoring all the others. How do we do it? Research by the British scientist Colin Cherry in the 1950s showed that we separate out individual voices by focusing on key characteristics – the speaker's gender, location and pitch. In 1958, British psychologist Donald Broadbent took this work to a new level with a theory of how the entire brain processes information. Up until then many psychologists believed that humans could only process one thing at a time. Broadbent showed that people could hear and comprehend more than one set of sounds simultaneously – provided they were simple enough. In a classic experiment, Broadbent asked people to listen to two sets of digits (such as '659', '842', and so on), one set played in each ear. Even though the numbers were played at the same time, listeners grouped the digits played through each ear rather than mixing them together. However, once the signals become too complex, a 'bottleneck' forms, making the signals impossible to manage simultaneously, which is part of the reason it's dangerous to drive while talking on the phone or texting.

3-SECOND PSYCHE
We are constantly bombarded with sounds, sights and other sensations – yet we can make sense of it all by focusing on small chunks of information.

3-MINUTE ANALYSIS
Broadbent's original theory said signals that didn't make it through the bottleneck were simply lost. However, in 1960, British psychologist Anne Treisman noted that Broadbent's theory couldn't account for the fact that people engrossed in complex tasks could still respond to the sound of their names. Treisman argued that unprocessed signals were actually retained, allowing especially dramatic or important signals to gain our attention.

3-SECOND BIOGRAPHIES
DONALD BROADBENT
1926–1993

COLIN CHERRY
1914–1979

ANNE TREISMAN
1935–

30-SECOND TEXT
Dave Munger

If we didn't have some kind of filter, we'd be caught in a perpetual storm of sensory information.

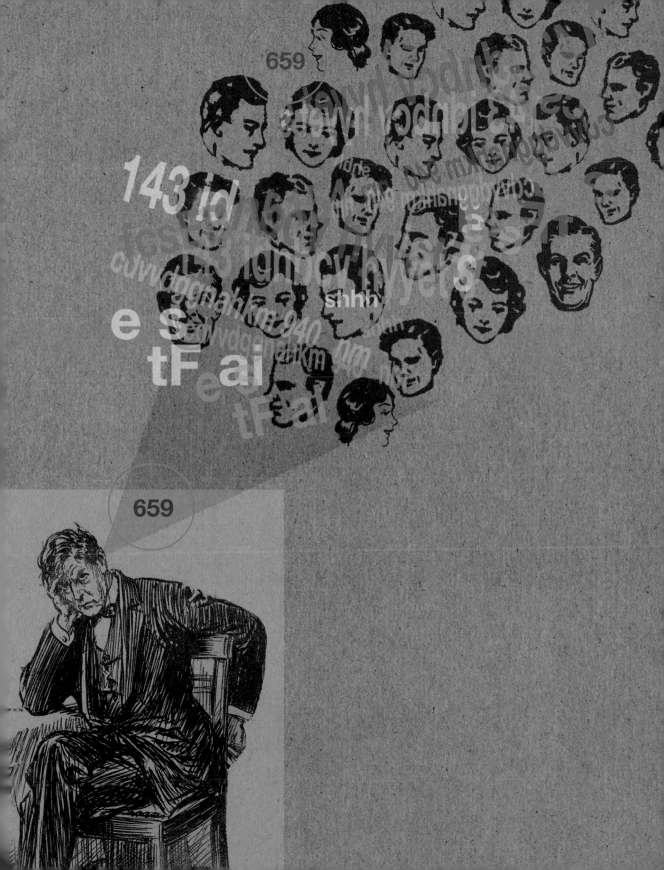

MILLER'S SEVEN

the 30-second theory

Quick, try to memorize this sequence of letters: UPSBMWCIAIOC. It's a daunting task until you notice that it's actually made up of four well-known acronyms: UPS and BMW are companies, and CIA and IOC are organizations. Without breaking the sequence of twelve letters into chunks, you'd have a hard time remembering them all. In 1956, US psychologist George Miller noticed that, although we can remember tens of thousands of items over the long term, the limit for short-term memory tasks such as this one seems to fall consistently around seven items – whether they are numbers, letters, words or even musical tones. But amazingly, Miller's student, Sidney Smith, was able to teach himself to recall forty random binary digits (zeros and ones) by combining them into chunks eight digits long. Each sequence of digits was like a separate 'word' to Smith, so he could remember many more digits than an untrained person. Similarly, we can remember long telephone numbers by chunking the digits into groups. We can quickly learn songs by chunking words into lines and rhyming pairs of lines – and the number of chunks that we can recall over the short term, Miller found, is nearly always very close to seven.

RELATED THEORIES
See also
THE COGNITIVE REVOLUTION
Page 22
BROADBENT'S BOTTLENECK
Page 146

3-SECOND BIOGRAPHIES
NELSON COWAN
1951–

GEORGE MILLER
1920–

30-SECOND TEXT
Dave Munger

3-SECOND PSYCHE
Under ordinary circumstances, we can remember about seven items at a time – but if we group them together into 'chunks', we can remember many more.

3-MINUTE ANALYSIS
While Miller's work is quite robust, recent studies have questioned it. Are you really remembering seven chunks, or are you just grouping those chunks into even bigger chunks? In 2001, American psychologist Nelson Cowan argued that the capacity of short-term memory is much less than seven. When we are prevented from making new chunks by working simultaneously on another task, the number of chunks that we can remember is closer to four.

The astonishing feats of performers at the annual World Memory Championships show how mnemonics can be used to extend short-term memory way beyond just seven items.

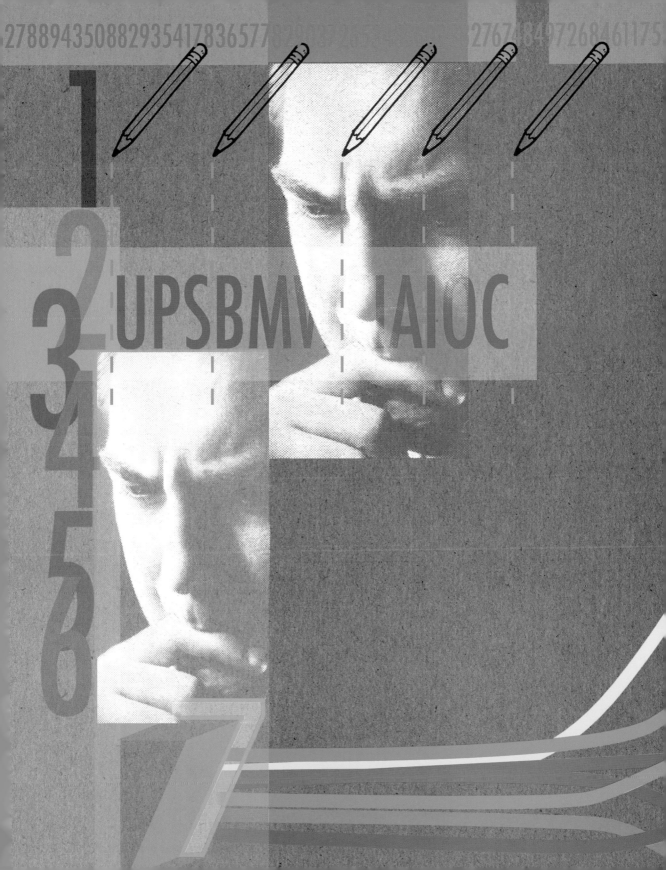

CONSCIOUSNESS

the 30-second theory

We all know what it means to be conscious, but an adequate definition of consciousness remains elusive. The contents of consciousness consist of a narrow, dynamic stream of everything we are presently aware of – our perceptions of the external world and bodily sensations, together with our thoughts, actions, emotions and memories. The contents of consciousness are commonly studied by using brain scanning to compare the brain's responses to stimuli that enter awareness with those that do not. A common framework for studying these phenomena is the global workspace theory, proposed by Bernard Baars in 1987, which likens consciousness to a working theatre. The vast majority of neural events are unconscious processes taking place 'behind the scenes', but some enter into conscious awareness – the 'stage' – when they become the focus of an attentional spotlight. The spotlight is surrounded by a fringe of vaguely conscious but crucial events, and acts as a hub which both distributes important information globally and is directed by the unconscious processes taking place behind the scenes. Viewed in this way, consciousness can be thought of as a means by which the brain prioritizes, and gives us access to, the information needed for healthy functioning.

RELATED THEORY
See also
MILLER'S SEVEN
Page 148

3-SECOND BIOGRAPHY
BERNARD BAARS
1950–

30-SECOND TEXT
Moheb Costandi

3-SECOND PSYCHE
A 'spotlight of attention' shines a bright beam on certain neural processes, which then enter into conscious awareness.

3-MINUTE ANALYSIS
Consciousness has long been the subject of debate among neuroscientists and philosophers. Modern brain research is just beginning to provide some understanding of it, and the global workspace theory is the most useful model for interpreting the available evidence. This approach has already provided valuable insight into disorders of consciousness such as coma and the persistent vegetative state, and some suggest that conditions such as schizophrenia involve a profound alteration of processing in the global workspace.

Although science is beginning to reveal the neural correlates of consciousness, quite how the wet tissue of the brain gives rise to the immaterial mind remains as elusive as ever.

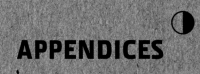

APPENDICES

RESOURCES

BOOKS

Eye and Brain
Richard L. Gregory
(Oxford University Press, 1997)

The Head Trip: Adventures on the Wheel of Consciousness
Jeff Warren
(Random House, 2007)

The History of Psychology: Fundamental Questions
Margaret P. Munger (editor)
(Oxford University Press, 2003)

How the Mind Works
Steven Pinker
(Allen Lane, 1998)

How to Think Straight About Psychology
Keith E. Stanovich
(Pearson Education, 2009)

Into the Silent Land: Travels in Neuropsychology
Paul Broks
(Atlantic Books, 2004)

Irrationality
Stuart Sutherland
(Pinter & Martin Ltd, 2007)

The Language Instinct
Steven Pinker
(Harper Perennial Modern Classics, 1997)

Mind Hacks: Tips & Tools for Using Your Brain
Tom Stafford and Matt Webb
(O'Reilly, 2004)

Nature via Nurture: A Fantastic Romp Through 24 Hours in the Life of Your Brain
Matt Ridley
(Harper Perennial, 2004)

The Oxford Companion to the Mind
Richard L. Gregory
(Oxford University Press, 2004)

The Rough Guide to Psychology
Christian Jarrett
(Penguin, 2011)

Social Psychology: The Second Edition
Roger Brown
(Simon & Schuster, 1985)

This Book Has Issues, Adventures in Popular Psychology
Christian Jarrett and Joannah Ginsburg
(Continuum, 2008)

MAGAZINES/JOURNALS

Psychological Science
http://psychologicalscience.org

The Psychologist
www.thepsychologist.org.uk

Scientific American Mind
http://www.scientificamerican.com/
sciammind/

WEBSITES

BPS Research Digest
www.researchdigest.org.uk/blog
A highly readable summary of the latest
psychology research.

Classics in the History of Psychology
http://psychclassics.yorku.ca/index.htm
An online repository of hundreds of
documents by renowned psychologists
from Allport to Lovelace to Wundt.

Frontal Cortex
http://www.wired.com/wiredscience/
frontal-cortex/
Fascinating psychology and neuroscience
insights from Jonah Lehrer, author of
How We Decide.

Mind Hacks
http://mindhacks.com/
Fascinating insights on psychology research
and news, with links to great psychology
articles and blog posts across the web.

Neurophilosophy
http://scienceblogs.com/neurophilosophy/
Neurophilosophy is a weblog about
molecules, minds and everything in
between.

Project Implicit
https://implicit.harvard.edu/implicit/
Participate in new research about
unconscious stereotyping.

Research Blogging
http://researchblogging.org
Click on 'psychology' for the latest blog
posts about recent peer-reviewed
psychology research.

Test Your Morals
http://www.yourmorals.org/
Test your own morals at this site run
by psychologist Jonathan Haidt and
his colleagues.

Track Your Happiness
http://www.trackyourhappiness.org/
Take part in an iPhone-based happiness
research project. Run by Dan Gilbert,
author of *Stumbling on Happiness*.

NOTES ON CONTRIBUTORS

EDITOR

Christian Jarrett is an award-winning journalist for *The Psychologist* magazine, published by the British Psychological Society, and he edits and writes the society's internationally renowned Research Digest blog (www.researchdigest.org.uk/blog). Christian also authored *The Rough Guide to Psychology* (2011), co-authored *This Book Has Issues, Adventures in Popular Psychology* (2008), contributed to *30-Second Theories* (2009) and has written for numerous publications including *The Times*, *Wired UK*, *BBC Focus* and *New Scientist*. He has a Ph.D. in Cognitive Neuroscience from the University of Manchester Institute of Science and Technology (UMIST). Christian tweets @Psych_Writer.

WRITERS

Vaughan Bell is a clinical psychologist who works between London in the UK and Medellín in Colombia. He is a Senior Research Fellow at the Institute of Psychiatry, King's College London and a clinical psychologist in the Department of Psychiatry at the University of Antioquia in Medellín. He also writes about the mind, brain and society for the press and the internet and is currently writing a book about hallucinations. Vaughan tweets @vaughanbell.

Moheb Costandi trained as a molecular and developmental neurobiologist and now works as a freelance science writer specializing in neuroscience. His work has been published in *BBC Focus Magazine*, *Technology Review*, *Scientific American* and *The Scientist*. He also writes regularly for *The Guardian*, and is the author of the highly regarded Neurophilosophy blog. Moheb tweets @mocost.

Dave Munger is Editor and co-founder of ResearchBlogging.org, a website collecting thousands of blog posts about peer-reviewed research, often written by experts in their fields. He writes a column on research blogging for seedmagazine.com. For five years he co-authored Cognitive Daily (scienceblogs.com/cognitivedaily), covering recent developments in psychology research. He has written or co-authored several textbooks, including *Researching Online* and *The Pocket Reader*. Dave tweets @davemunger.

Tom Stafford works as a lecturer in Psychology and Cognitive Science at the University of Sheffield. He co-authored *Mind Hacks: Tips and Tools for Using your Brain* (2004) and *The Rough Guide Book of Brain Training* (2010). His latest work is an ebook called *The Narrative Escape* (2010). Tom tweets @tomstafford.

INDEX

ACKNOWLEDGMENTS

PICTURE CREDITS
The publisher would like to thank the following individuals and organizations for their kind permission to reproduce the images in this book. Every effort has been made to acknowledge the pictures, however we apologize if there are any unintentional omissions.

Aaron T. Beck: 118.
Getty Images: 56; Hulton Archive: 20; AFP: 38.
Alexandra Milgram: 78.
Topfoto: 96.
UCI Communications: 142.